GOD,
I DON'T
UNDERSTAND

GOD,
I DON'T
UNDERSTAND

ANSWERS TO DIFFICULT
QUESTIONS OF THE FAITH

KENNETH BOA

Victor®

The Bible Teacher's Teacher

COOK COMMUNICATIONS MINISTRIES
Colorado Springs, Colorado • Paris, Ontario
KINGSWAY COMMUNICATIONS, LTD.
Eastbourne, England

Victor® is an imprint of
Cook Communications Ministries, Colorado Springs, CO 80918
Cook Communications, Paris, Ontario
Kingsway Communications, Eastbourne, England

GOD, I DON'T UNDERSTAND
© 1975, 2007 by Kenneth Boa

Also published under the title *Unraveling the Big Questions about God*.

First Printing, 2007
Printed in the United States of America

1 2 3 4 5 6 7 8 9 10

Cover Design: BMB Design, Inc.
Cover Photo: Royalty Free - © iStockphoto
Diagrams: Kenneth Boa and William Shell
Diagrams: Bob de la Peña

ISBN 978-0-78144-423-1

LCCN 2006932649

TO KAREN

Her worth is far above jewels.

—Proverbs 31:10 NASB

CONTENTS

List of Illustrations and Tables

FOREWORD

Here is good theology in understandable language. Not all writers can accomplish this. Either the theology is so diluted that it is not worth the time to read, or the language in which it is expressed is so complicated that it is unintelligible to ordinary mortals like most of us.

Ken Boa has written clearly about some very important subjects we ought to be thinking about. The author is one of those not-too-common students who stimulated me as a teacher. I recall with pleasure many provocative conversations with him in and out of the classroom. His range of knowledge, thoughtful approach to problems, and clear explanations, which I enjoyed during those times together, are clearly displayed in this book.

Each chapter makes its own particular contribution to stretching our minds. I wanted to add "but don't miss the ones on sovereignty versus responsibility or space or the Bible," but if I say that, I hope no one will think the other chapters are somehow less important, for that is not so.

It is a pleasure to commend this book for reading and study. The investment of time will pay good dividends.

—Charles C. Ryrie

INTRODUCTORY
NOTES

The primary assumption underlying this book is that the Bible is God's revelation to humanity. These pages do not endorse the "just take it by faith" attitude. It is beyond this book's scope to present the evidence for this assumption. Many other works, such as F. F. Bruce's *The New Testament Documents: Are They Reliable?* and John W. Montgomery's *History and Christianity*, deal with the issue.

—KB

THIRTY YEARS LATER

God, I Don't Understand was my first book, and I wrote it in 1974 when I was twenty-nine years old. It was published by Victor in 1975 and later published by Zondervan under the title *Unraveling the Big Questions about God*. Victor has decided to republish this book in its classic form. Therefore, I've left the book largely as it was originally written. I attempted to build this book on the foundation of God's timeless truth, and changes I'd make today are not substantive but ancillary. I hope this book's republication will edify a new generation of readers and enhance their capacity to worship by stretching their minds about the glory, greatness, goodness, and grace of the infinite and personal God.

In brief "Thirty Years Later" comments at the end of each chapter, I'll mention some thoughts and issues I would address if I were writing the book now.

The Victor Leaders Guide by William Shell contained a number of diagrams that appear in this book.

I made some additions and changes in the *Unraveling the Big Questions about God* edition, and these are part of this manuscript. I also added several slight editorial corrections to this edition.

Much of what we now call noninclusive language was originally inclusive. Younger readers are largely unaware of this understanding, so it is important to emphasize that when I used words like "man" and "mankind" in 1974 I used them as they were universally understood until the late twentieth century—as inclusive of all people, not merely males.

The wealth of Christian apologetics literature in the last thirty years would lead to new recommendations. Some of my own books in this area are *I'm Glad You Asked, Faith Has Its Reasons*, and *20 Compelling Evidences That God Exists*.

The last thirty years have seen unprecedented and accelerating cultural, social, and technological changes that have dramatically reshaped the contours of worldview and lifestyle. Postmodernism's runaway relativism has created widespread skepticism about objective truth and unchanging absolutes. Authority is less grounded in revelation, tradition, and reason; these are being replaced by subjective feelings and opinions. Thus, this book's assumption of biblical inspiration is rapidly becoming more countercultural and an object of increasing hostility. Pluralism and secularization now abound. Tolerance has been redefined to mean acceptance, and people are being taught that it is intolerant to disagree with a person's beliefs and/or behavior. Ironically, this has led to increasing hostility toward those who disagree with this definition of tolerance.

Contemporary Christians have been profoundly affected by these changes, and an increasing number of self-proclaimed followers of Christ uncritically embrace a relativistic perspective on the true, the good, and the beautiful.

Biblical illiteracy has greatly increased over the last thirty years, and people are more ungrounded in biblical content, thought patterns, and theology. Therefore, the issues and arguments in this book may be generally less accessible to contemporary readers.

Nevertheless, we now have access to an unparalleled abundance of excellent written, audio, video, and Internet resources that provide cogent evidences for the authority of God's revelatory Word and for the superior coherence, comprehensiveness, and consistency of the theistic worldview.

Thirty years is but a blip in human history, and human nature has not changed; people are still searching for answers to life's same fundamental questions.

Chapter 1

WHAT'S THE PROBLEM?

Most people seem to pass through this short life without ever stopping to consider how profound and mysterious the universe really is. We throw around terms like *energy, time, space, gravity,* and *matter* as though we really understand what they mean. We get into our life routines and take things for granted, asking few questions. But underlying all this, a tremendous uncertainty—and often a deep desire to find some solid ground—exists.

On the other hand, millions have discovered the joy of satisfied desire—they've found and touched the solid ground. It comes as a priceless gift, free to all who will receive it.

If a powerful being suddenly appeared, offered you a strange box, and claimed that it contained the answers to many of the universe's secrets, would you be interested? Assuming you could overcome your impulse to run and you knew the creature wasn't diabolical, you'd probably be quite anxious to look into the box. After all, who wouldn't like to learn the mysteries of the cosmos and discover the blueprints for life if they were so readily available?

The living God has done even more for us than this hypothetical being with the box. He's given us a written revelation that we can keep, examine, study, and share. God loves us so much that he chose to let us in on some eternal secrets of the universe. The Bible, God's revelation, lets us know *why we exist and how we should live.*

Today we still seek answers to questions raised since antiquity: Who am I? Where did I come from and where am I going? Are there any absolutes? Apart from God's revelation—his Word—the quest for these answers is futile.

The pursuit of philosophy has led men to antiphilosophy, cynicism, and despair. Men of great intellectual ability find little ground for agreement because their solutions are only speculations. Their answers to the basic questions are simply descents into a pool of unfounded faith.

People hunger for meaning in life. That hunger is unsatisfied, even aggravated, by vain attempts to find meaning in the occult, mysticism, analysis, philosophy, and introspection. Due to our sinful pride, it's difficult for us to receive anything from God simply as a free gift. When God tells us the real questions and answers are in the Bible, it offends our pride. It sounds too easy. We'd rather discover the hidden knowledge, the answers of the elite. Egotistically, we hope life's profundities can be mastered by unaided human reasoning.

Those of us who know the Lord Jesus Christ are persuaded that he has the words of eternal life. By his grace we have finally realized that the answers to the basic questions of life have been revealed and a relationship with the living God is available to all as a free gift. One of the last things Moses said before his death was, "The secret things belong to the LORD our God, but the things revealed belong to us and to our children forever" (Deut. 29:29).

The person who believes God's Word doesn't commit intellectual suicide. Instead, his mind rises to heights he previously could not have attained. He receives supernatural revelation from an all-knowing Creator. When we start with the Bible as a foundation for truth and build upon this, our reasoning is not stifled but stimulated. We are encouraged by the Author of life to erect our superstructures in all disciplines, including science, psychology, and art—but to do so on the foundation of biblical truth.

SPECULATION OR AUTHORITY

It's important for us to start with the proper assumptions or presuppositions about life. No matter how wonderful and consistent a system may seem, if it is built upon false premises, the entire edifice is doomed to destruction. The Christian doesn't build on others' speculations but on God's revelation. His presupposition about life is profoundly simple: "I believe that God has revealed himself to men, and that revelation is the Bible." Everything he believes about mankind, evil, the future of the universe, God, and salvation comes out of this one presupposition. The child of God begins with the idea that truth is what God says about a thing and that what he has said is in the Bible.

When we start with this simple presupposition, we are released from the limits and uncertainty of our own poor wisdom. We can joyfully allow God's greater wisdom to direct our steps (see 1 Cor. 1:21, 25). The Christian realizes he's started with something intellectually greater than himself. Thus, he has freedom to examine the world and all that is in it, being confidently assured of who made it, how it got here, and why.

The wonderful thing about God's revelation is that he couches infinite truth in finite language. The Bible, like its Author, can never bore the one who studies it carefully, because it will take an eternity to search out its heights and depths.

The infinite depth of truth is possible because God, not man, initiated the process. The apostle Peter made this clear when he wrote that "No prophecy of Scripture came about by the prophet's own interpretation. For prophecy never had its origin in the will of man, but men spoke from God as they were carried along by the Holy Spirit" (2 Peter 1:20–21).

God tells us we should expect the revelation from him—the infinite, omniscient Creator—also to be infinitely deep. "'For my thoughts are not your thoughts, neither are your ways my ways,' declares the LORD. 'As the heavens are higher than the earth, so are my ways higher than your ways and my thoughts than your thoughts'" (Isa. 55:8–9).

IT'S BEYOND US

It follows that we cannot and should not expect to understand the Bible exhaustively. If we could, the Bible wouldn't be divine but limited to human intelligence. This leads to a very important idea over which many non-Christians and even Christians stumble: *Since the Bible is an infinite revelation, it often brings the reader beyond the limit of his intelligence.*

As simple as the Bible's message of sin and of free salvation through Christ is, an incredible subtlety and profundity underlies all its doctrines. Even a child can receive Christ as his Savior, thereby appropriating the free gift of eternal life. Yet no philosopher has more than scratched the surface regarding what happened at the cross. The Bible forces any reader to crash into the ceiling of his own comprehension. Beyond this he cannot go until he sees the Lord face-to-face.

Until a person recognizes that his own wisdom and intelligence are not enough, he is not ready to listen to God's greater wisdom. Jesus alluded to this when he said to God, "You have hidden these things from the wise and learned, and revealed them to little children" (Luke 10:21).

Contrast a dog's mental ability with that of a human. The dog is able to handle a limited number of bits of information. A human also has mental limits but is capable of storing and working with a good deal more information than his dog.

There is some overlap between the dog's mental faculties and those of a human. The dog may be able to relate to its master's eating food, but, no doubt, has a great deal more difficulty trying to understand what its master is doing when he keeps staring at pieces of paper and slowly turning the pages of a book. Though a dog can't relate to many of the things its owner does, there is enough common ground for limited communication, and a human can teach his pet. There's also enough common ground for a human to love a dog without having a condescending attitude.

This overlap is very important, especially regarding communication. It is almost impossible for anyone to love or train something like a worm or a leech. Why? Because there is no communication.

When a human does something beyond an animal's comprehension, it must remain a mystery to that animal since it has no categories it can use to correlate this behavior. A dog can be taught to fetch the morning newspaper, but it is another matter to teach it how to read it.

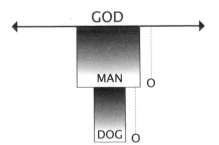

God is infinitely more above a human in his knowledge and comprehension than a human is above a dog. Even so, areas of communication exist between God and a human as they do between a human and a dog. However, man often does things beyond the comprehension of the animal and God beyond the understanding of people.

The corresponding analogy between a human and God is valid as well. However, the gap is even greater because we must compare a human's finite mental capacity to the Lord's boundless capacity. Even so, God can still communicate real truth to us, and we can communicate with him, though on a limited level. As Francis Schaeffer pointed out, God has communicated truly, though not exhaustively, to men. He can comprehend a myriad of things that we cannot grasp. Since the Bible is God's revelation to man, it should not be surprising that it implies or directly states some of these areas.

THE MYSTERIES OF GOD

We need to find a name for such revealed incomprehensibles. The word *paradox* isn't the best choice, because it often implies only an *apparent* contradiction. *Paradox* is often used for a semantic or a verbal contradiction. In this case, we can change the words to eliminate the contradiction.

One scriptural example of such a paradox is Paul's statement, "When I am weak, then I am strong" (2 Cor. 12:10). The paradox can be resolved by rewording it: "The less I have, the more I depend on him" (TLB).

The word *oxymoron* is also inappropriate since it's simply a combination of two contradictory or incongruous words (*heavy lightness* or *cruel kindness*). This is more a literary device than a description of two contradictory concepts that cannot both be true at once.

We need a word to describe the fact that God's revelation to man sometimes goes beyond the level of human reasoning and comprehension by stating as fact two things that men cannot reconcile. The word *antinomy* comes closer to describing these phenomena in God's Word. Webster defines *antinomy* as "a contradiction between two equally valid principles or between inferences correctly drawn from such principles."

This word's two parts—*anti* (against) and *nomos* (law)—simply mean "against the law" of human reasoning. What is quite comprehensible to God may be "antinomial" to man. Some things in the Scriptures may be difficult to comprehend, others may be obvious antinomies, and still others may only be possible antinomies.

In the original version of this book, I used *antinomy* throughout to describe the things in the Bible that go beyond or against human reason. However, some people found this term confusing, and a few readers with philosophical backgrounds thought I was using *antinomy* the way that Immanuel Kant used this word. (Kant argued that certain religious concepts were *ultimately* contradictory and could never be otherwise. That is not this book's position.) Things revealed in Scripture that seem incomprehensible to the human mind are fully comprehended by the divine mind. They are "superrational," not irrational.

To overcome this possible confusion, I've decided to substitute the word *mystery* for *antinomy*. Mystery comes from the Greek word *mysterion*, used in the New Testament for "secret" or "secret teaching." *Mystery* in Scripture often refers to something that was previously hidden but is now revealed. For example, in 1 Corinthians 15:51, Paul writes, "Listen, I tell you a mystery: We will not all sleep, but we will all be changed." God revealed to Paul that believers who are alive when the Lord returns won't see physical death but will be changed "in the twinkling of an eye" from a mortal body to an immortal resurrected body. According to the apostle, the statement that "one out of one dies" will one day prove false.

In this book, the word mystery *will refer to those truths in Scripture that are beyond the boundary of human understanding.* Two of the more obvious mysteries that will be considered in this book are the Trinity and the divine/human nature of Jesus Christ.

Mysteries are relative, not absolute. What is a mystery to a dog may be quite comprehensible to a man, and what is mysterious to human reasoning may be comprehensible to beings with greater reasoning powers (angels and God).

Because Christ conquered sin and death, the degeneration of man and the universe due to man's fall will be reversed when he comes again. We'll gain more ability to comprehend God's truth, and it's likely that we'll understand many things that are now mysteries. "Now we see but a poor reflection as in a mirror; then we shall see face to face. Now I know in part; then I shall know fully, even as I am fully known" (1 Cor. 13:12).

BEWARE OF EXPLANATIONS

It is important to remember that, because of its very nature, *we cannot illustrate or explain a mystery.* When we're working with a real mystery, even good illustrations will fall short of complete clarification. Accepting such explanations as complete can lead to error and a lack of balance. While illustrations may help clarify two ideas that appear on a human level to be contradictory, they should not be given with the impression that they will provide an adequate solution to the riddle itself.

The believer, therefore, must realize his need for faith in God's revealed Word. He must place his human wisdom in a position subordinate to God's revelation. It would be the height of egotism for a person to say that because an idea in the Bible doesn't make sense (doesn't conform to his or her reasoning), it can't be true and the Bible must be in error on this point. Yet people try to judge the Bible instead of letting it judge them. They try to approach God on their own terms, wanting to tell him how to operate and who to be.

When a person insists on trying to subject two contradictory elements of a biblical mystery to human comprehension, he will inevitably, though perhaps subtly, move to one extreme or to the other. The only way to rationalize a mystery is to remove the tension between the two contradictory elements by essentially ignoring one or the other. Either we'll enlarge idea A out of proportion and minimize idea B, or vice versa.

We need to understand both elements in each mystery while resisting our natural temptation to remove the tension. To maintain proper balance, we should accept the tension by supporting both ideas equally. This, of course, is unnatural, and it is here that faith in God's revealed Word must govern us.

It's not a cop-out to accept both ideas of a biblical mystery by faith without continually looking for some rationalization or explanation. It would only be a cop-out if we were dealing with a difficult theological concept rather than a mystery. It's important, therefore, to distinguish between the two to determine how to approach a given problem.

Mysteries require precise statement and analysis. The improper choice of a word or phrase could introduce an error by overemphasizing one of the two ideas involved in the mystery. This is true of all theology, since the words used (even so-called insignificant words) will sometimes affect large meanings. This is not a matter of wrangling over words, but simply the nature of theology.

This preciseness of language can be found throughout the Scriptures, since God inspired not only the ideas but also the words. For example, Paul builds a whole argument on the ending of one word from an Old Testament reference (see Gal. 3:16).

TRUTH IS COMPLEX

Another interesting thing about mysteries is they seem to touch on every major area of theology. In fact, an examination of mysteries is simply a different way of looking at theology.

This does not mean the basic doctrines of Scripture aren't clear, for they certainly are. The biblical account of the origin of sin; the nature of God as an omniscient, sovereign, eternal Being; the details of the Lord's creative and redemptive work; and humanity's ultimate future are all clearly spelled out.

However, these very doctrines and others, when more closely examined, show a tremendous subtlety and complexity that can defy analysis. Behind all these doctrines is a simple yet immensely complex reality.

We also can observe this same complexity in nature, because everything that exists derives its being from God himself. The Scriptures say of Jesus, "All things were created by him and for him. He is before all things, and in him all things hold together" (Col. 1:16–17).

An in-depth study of any part of God's creation illustrates this complexity. Things that appear to be clear and simple display astonishing depths of intricacy. The more closely we examine a flower or a leaf, the more marvelous it becomes. Thus, a study of the mysterious things of God's written revelation can be both profitable and humbling. It can lead to a greater awe and appreciation of the One who allows all who believe in him to be members of his own household.

HERESY RESULTS FROM OVERSIMPLIFICATION

Another reason to study the mysteries of Scripture is to avoid the misunderstandings that result in false teaching. Wrong theology and many heretical cults have arisen over the centuries from a lack of balance with respect to mysteries. False teaching results when people stumble over important mysteries, such as the Trinity and God-man, without recognizing them as such.

When a person encounters a mystery, he may try to avoid it instead of acknowledging it for what it is. He refuses to believe that both concepts contained within the mystery are true at once, thinking that if something doesn't make sense to natural logic, it certainly can't be true. This idea becomes the foundation stone for erroneous doctrinal systems. The error generally consists in overemphasizing one concept at the expense of its counterpart.

Another common solution people use to avoid mysteries is the convenient adjustment of their method of Bible interpretation. That is, if the ideas contained in scriptural passages do not make sense based on a normal literal interpretation, some people spiritualize or allegorize the passages involved. They simply refuse to acknowledge the text's obvious meaning because it doesn't fit with their preconceived notions. Mysteries are therefore closely related to Bible interpretation because carelessness in one will produce carelessness in the other.

The Jehovah's Witnesses are an example of how trying to rationalize or avoid biblical mysteries produces false teaching and cultism. They reject the doctrine of the Trinity because it doesn't make sense to them that God could be three persons and yet one God in essence. This admittedly runs against the grain of human reasoning, and a natural human tendency would be to avoid the problem by holding a unitarian view of God.

The simple reasoning involved is that since God is one he cannot consist of three persons. The next step then is to impose this viewpoint upon all Scripture, twisting it to avoid the fact of the deity and/or personality of Jesus Christ and the Holy Spirit. In this case, as in many others, the refusal to accept what is by nature a mystery has led directly to serious errors in interpretation and theology.

Sensitivity to the implications of biblical mysteries can be both corrective medicine and preventive medicine. It can correct false teaching by providing a more open and less biased approach to the Scriptures. It can also prevent the encroachment of error by helping people understand why and how error slips in unnoticed.

A MARK OF DIVINITY

The fact that the Bible contains genuine mysteries is good evidence of its divine origin. If it were not inspired of God, its teachings would be limited to human intelligence, imagination, and reason.

The question then arises: What about scriptures from other religions? Religious books like the Qur'an (Islam) and the Bhagavad Gita (Hinduism) and cultic books like the Book of Mormon (Mormonism) and *Science and*

Health (Christian Science) contain few true mysteries—in some cases, none. Some of these books, in fact, rehash the Bible to remove the biblical mysteries because of the difficulties they produce. Other scriptures like to get rid of things like the Trinity, the God-man, and the problem of divine sovereignty versus human responsibility. They include paradoxical notions to build a fabric of the enigmatic, but these notions don't ultimately defy human reasoning.

The wonderful and unique thing about the Bible is that it is full of what people would never have dreamed up. Many of its messages are the last things people would want to write. The fact is that mysteries by their very nature produce insoluble problems—just the sort of problems that would keep people from considering the Bible at all apart from a supernatural intervention.

However, we must be very careful here, because this is not to say that the things revealed in God's Word are illogical. All the ideas that can be comprehended in the Bible make wonderful sense. But other concepts, while not contrary to human reason, do go beyond it. The Bible frequently shows evidence of a logic and understanding far superior to anything presently attainable by mankind.

A Tool for Apologetics

Mysteries' apologetic value is another practical reason for their study because their presence in the Bible relates to some of the non-Christian objections to Christianity. This type of study can help us more clearly understand why non-Christians may have trouble with the message of the Gospels. We begin to see how absolutely important it is to rely on the Holy Spirit's convicting ministry when witnessing to those who don't know the Savior.

Some mysteries have more practical value to everyday Christian life and witnessing than others. Two that affect us directly are those dealing with the problem of evil and the nature of salvation.

Other mysteries seem to be more abstract, not relating closely to everyday life. Because of this, they don't cause as many problems and are easily acceptable. Most people have fewer difficulties with the nature of time and the resurrection body than they do with divine sovereignty versus human freedom and responsibility. But since these concepts are equally mysterious, Christians should remember that the ones they find harder to accept are actually no more difficult than the ones that do not bother them.

SEVEN REASONS FOR STUDYING MYSTERIES

There are at least seven practical reasons to study the Bible's mysteries:

1. *To show human reason must be subject to God's revelation.* A strong faith in all Scripture is essential; it's the only way to achieve intellectual satisfaction about the difficult portions of God's Word.
2. *To maintain balance in critical areas of biblical theology* and, in fact, provide a different perspective to theological study.
3. *To gain a greater appreciation for God and his Word* by seeing something of the profound depth and ineffable mysteries involved. This is very humbling for the child of God and should result in praise and worship of our eternal Father.
4. *To get insight into the growth of false teaching* through the centuries and learn how it can be, and should have been, avoided. Such study also illustrates the need for a proper and consistent interpretation of the Bible.
5. *To realize the Scriptures' uniqueness and divine origin.*
6. *To gain a valuable aid in witnessing to non-Christians,* because mysteries' existence and the problems they cause to the natural mind underlie some of unbelievers' objections to Christianity.
7. *To reap practical value for the daily Christian walk.* This study can affect a believer's outlook on life and therefore his behavior.

One danger to avoid is discovering mysteries where they don't really exist. We can search so hard for mysteries that we exaggerate mere difficulties to the level of true mystery as defined in this book. Some subjects included in this study as mysteries may be debatable and are so labeled, primarily the chapter on space (the creation). This is a possible mystery, but not dogmatically classified as such. It has been included because considering it may be helpful and consistent with our purpose.

It is important to realize that just because something is called a mystery it does not mean that we may nonchalantly set it aside without further thought or discussion. This could lead to a pious "just take it by faith" attitude, when in reality these subjects demand continued thought and periodic reevaluation.

Just as one or more of the subjects discussed in this study may not absolutely be mysterious, there may be (and probably are) genuine biblical mysteries that haven't been included.

An appreciation of the wonders of God's revelation can lead to a greater comprehension of the Bible's uniqueness, wisdom, and depth and, correspondingly, of the One who inspired it. This subject relates directly to the two great works God has done for which he deserves and is to receive all praise, honor, worship, and dominion forevermore: his loving work of creation and his redemption of that creation.

> Sing to the LORD a new song;
> sing to the LORD, all the earth.
> Sing to the LORD, praise his name;
> proclaim his salvation day after day.
> Declare his glory among the nations,
> his marvelous deeds among all peoples.
>
> For great is the LORD and most worthy of praise;
> he is to be feared above all gods.
> For all of the gods of the nations are idols,
> but the LORD made the heavens.
> Splendor and majesty are before him;
> strength and glory are in his sanctuary. (Ps. 96:1–6)
>
> To him who sits on the throne and to the Lamb
> be praise and honor and glory and power,
> for ever and ever! (Rev. 5:13)
>
> Now to the King eternal, immortal, invisible, the only God,
> be honor and glory for ever and ever. Amen. (1 Tim. 1:17)

THIRTY YEARS LATER

- Christianity's uniqueness impresses me as important evidence for its truth. Apart from revelation, no one could have thought up the gospel of salvation by grace through faith. Besides the unique scriptural mysteries presented in this book, a substantial list of other truths only found in biblical Christianity exists. Three examples: (1) Instead of humans sacrificing to God, he sacrifices and suffers on our behalf. (2) God's Word affirms both human dignity and human depravity. (3) Only the Bible gives value and meaning to human suffering.

- It requires a certain amount of knowledge to realize how ignorant we really are. Scripture's consistent message is the Lord telling us, "I am God, and you are not. I am the wellspring of all creation and of the true, the good, and the beautiful. Life is theocentric, not anthropocentric. You are called to the wisdom and satisfaction of radical trust in me and sacrificial obedience to what I command."

- Not much has changed in thirty years regarding the problem of human understanding and God's revelation. Despite advances in computers, the Internet, information storage, mathematics, astronomy, quantum theory, exploration of the oceans, and biology since 1974, the Bible's revelation remains fresh, and the limits of human understanding remain well defined.

- Living in an information age, we need to be more careful than ever not to believe that our finite comprehension and powers of memory have removed all mystery from creation. In fact, the opposite is true. The scientific discoveries in the last three decades reveal more mysteries in the created order than ever.

- We've become flooded with more information than previous generations even could conceive. Average people can readily access virtually every creative work of writing, music, science, and performance art from their home armchair, automobile, and laptop in minutes. But this torrent of information only further demonstrates how we need to appreciate what we do not understand and cannot grasp without God's help. It also means we need a moral compass now more than ever.

- Unlike software manufacturers, God will not and need not publish versions 2.0, 3.0, or 4.0. His Word is the only sure foundation in an unstable world.

- Faith isn't a logical certainty but a product of our relationship with the triune Father, Son, and Holy Spirit. Like all our relationships it is imperfect, but faith and doubt can coexist in tension that is relieved more and more as our relationship becomes more intimate. The key to the spiritual journey is growing trust.

- It requires a growing sense of humility and dependence on God to embrace the tensioned interplay of concepts that transcend human comprehension and subjective experience. "If anyone is willing to do His will, he will know of the teaching, whether it is of God or whether I speak from Myself" (John 7:17 NASB). There's a moral and spiritual prerequisite to receiving spiritual truth, since it consists "not in words taught by human wisdom, but in those taught by the Spirit, combining spiritual thoughts with spiritual words" (1 Cor. 2:13 NASB).

- Mystery goes against the grain of the human quest for autonomy, control, and measurement. As we grow in the faith, we must move away from pat answers to a willingness to accept ambiguity and uncertainty. A growing sense of wonder and childlike trust, gratitude, and awe should accompany the journey of spiritual formation.

- In our heavenly life to come, three possibilities await us: (1) Some mysteries may be instantly clarified. (2) Some mysteries may be clarified over time. (3) Some mysteries may have partial resolution but lack complete resolution forever. We will never be able to plumb the infinite abyss of the Mystery we call God, and we will never know him as he knows himself.

Chapter 2

THE GOD-MAN

J esus Christ himself, the central figure of Christianity, is really a biblical mystery. Many portions of Scripture completely affirm his deity, showing that at no time did he lose his divine nature. Yet the Bible teaches, equally strongly, that Christ became fully human.

HIS DEITY

The Word of God gives Christ divine titles. The familiar first words of the gospel of John read, "In the beginning was the Word, and the Word was with God, and *the Word was God.*" John makes it clear that this Word is Jesus Christ: "The Word became flesh and made his dwelling among us. We have seen his glory, the glory of the One and Only, who came from the Father, full of grace and truth" (John 1:14). Jesus Christ is therefore called God in John 1:1.

The same is true of this passage: "But about the Son he says, 'Your throne, *O God,* will last for ever and ever, and righteousness will be the scepter of your kingdom'" (Heb. 1:8).

Paul addresses Christ as God when he says, "While we wait for the blessed hope—the glorious appearing of our great God and Savior, Jesus Christ" (Titus 2:13; see 2 Peter 1:1).

The gospel of John records Thomas's response to the resurrected Christ: "Thomas said to him, 'My Lord and my God!'" (20:28).

Jesus is called the Son of God in numerous passages (Luke 3:22; Matt. 16:15–17; John 10:36). He is also called Lord in many passages (1 Cor. 12:3; Phil. 2:11).

Jesus not only accepted but also demanded worship due only to God (John 5:23). Christ claimed to be the supreme object of faith, demanding of men the same kind of faith they placed in God (John 17:1–3). He said, "I and the Father are one" (John 10:30).

The scriptural case for Jesus Christ as God is further supported by Christ's divine attributes and words. He is eternal (John 17:5; Heb. 1:11–12), omnipresent (Matt. 28:20), and omnipotent (Heb. 1:3). The Scriptures show him to be the Creator of all things (John 1:3; Col. 1:16; Heb. 1:2) and the one who holds all things in the universe together (Col. 1:17; Heb. 1:3). He alone, as God, offers forgiveness of sins (Luke 5:20–24), and all men will face him in judgment (John 5:24–28). The fact of Christ's full deity has clear biblical support.

HIS HUMANITY

The Bible builds an equally clear case to support Jesus' full humanity subsequent to the incarnation. Christ had a human birth (Matt. 1:18–25; Luke 2:4–21; John 1:14; 1 Tim. 3:16; 1 John 4:2) and human development (Luke 2:52). He had all the human elements: a body (John 2:21), a soul (John 12:27 NASB), and a spirit (Luke 23:46).

Also, just as Christ had divine names, he had human names such as "man" (1 Tim. 2:5), "Son of Man" (Luke 19:10), and "Son of David" (Mark 10:47). Christ possessed all human limitations except sin: He got tired, hungry, thirsty, sorrowful; and he died.

The Bible, therefore, gives clear testimony to the humanity as well as the complete deity of Jesus Christ. Paul summarizes this: "For in Christ all the fullness of the Deity lives in bodily form" (Col. 2:9).

The mystery here lies in the fact that humanity is not the same as deity. If Jesus were 50 percent God and 50 percent man (as some have taught), there would be no problem, since one-half plus one-half equals one. But the Bible doesn't allow this because it testifies that Jesus is a total man and fully God.

Even though it's easy to make a statement like this, there is no way to truly comprehend it, because one plus one does not equal one. It's like trying to put one quart of water and one quart of oil into a one-quart container.

Human reasoning denies that one can be fully human and fully divine, but the Bible tells us that's the case with Jesus Christ.

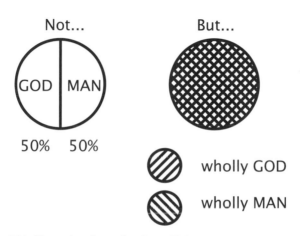

The GOD–MAN

This illustration shows that Jesus Christ is not 50 percent God and 50 percent man, but wholly God and wholly man at the same time as one person.

THREE ALTERNATIVES

When someone realizes the Scriptures reveal Christ to be the complete God-man, he has three basic alternatives. First, he may decide to reject this revelation because it doesn't make sense to him. Such a rejection would diminish or completely erase the Word of God's authority in his mind.

Second, he can try to reason it out, reword it, or illustrate it, as though it could be resolved like a paradox. In this case, people skirt the issue by minimizing certain Scriptures or avoiding a direct collision with the biblical data's implications on this point.

The third alternative is to acknowledge that no analogies or illustrations will really solve the puzzle and that the complete authority of the Word of God must be recognized, no matter how difficult some of its implications may be. All the biblical data is accepted by faith, and reason is made subject to revelation. Only when the Bible is approached in this way can intellectual satisfaction be attained.

There's a parallel to this in salvation: A person without Christ will not rid himself of his doubts about Christianity until he decides to receive Christ into his life by faith. Satisfaction and peace then follow as a natural by-product.

It's unfortunate that, historically, most people confronted by this mystery have chosen one of the first two alternatives. They've either rejected the biblical testimony concerning the God-man or juggled or ignored certain passages to make this compatible with human comprehension. This has led to two inevitable extremes.

One extreme is to reject Jesus' deity, reducing him to the level of being a man only. Often people will try to soften the thrust of this approach by throwing in a few kind words, saying Jesus was indeed a "great teacher" or a "true prophet." Statements like these shouldn't fool anyone, since almost all false systems want to give lip service to Jesus and put him on their bandwagon in spite of their rejection of his deity.

The implications of this extreme undermine all of Christianity. If true, it would mean the Bible is not true and salvation is still not available, since the death of a mere man (no matter how noble he may have been) can't provide the infinite purchase price required to redeem other men from their sins. This would leave all of us in deep trouble, since none of us can hope to satisfy a holy God with our own efforts.

This first extreme viewpoint implies it's an utter waste of time to study the Scriptures and get into Christianity at all. If Christ isn't God, then the Bible is wrong, there is no salvation, and each person must become his own authority for "truth."

The opposite extreme is equally devastating. In this case, Christ's deity is affirmed but his humanity is minimized or rejected. Interestingly, the results of this extreme are essentially the same as those of the first. The Bible wouldn't be God's Word, and salvation wouldn't be available for men.

Since the Bible makes it clear Jesus Christ was completely human, rejecting his humanity is tantamount to a rejection of the Bible. And salvation wouldn't be available because the substitutionary atonement requires that Jesus Christ must die as a man to bear judgment for the sins of all men. As Scripture says, "There is one God and one mediator between God and men, the man Christ Jesus, who gave himself as a ransom for all men—the testimony given in its proper time" (1 Tim. 2:5–6). The Messiah could not have become the mediator between God and man apart from becoming the God-man by taking on human flesh. The notion that Christ never became a man would destroy many other important biblical doctrines, but the two discussed here (God's revelation to man and his provision of a Savior) are the most critical.

ERRORS THROUGH THE CENTURIES

Church history affords many illustrations of how people have tried either to reject or to rationalize this God-man mystery. The two erroneous extremes just discussed have appeared in many forms throughout the centuries and will continue to arise as long as people refuse to bow to the authority of God's revelation of himself in the Scriptures.

The Gnostics were among the first to pervert the biblical doctrine of the God-man. Due to their dualistic conviction that matter is evil, they refused to believe in the Incarnation. Theirs was a form of Docetism, a doctrine that taught Christ only *seemed* to have a real body. They believed that Christ tricked the evil god of the Old Testament at the crucifixion because his body wasn't real.

The apostle John fought against the developing Gnosticism of his day and urged his readers to "test the spirits," for "every spirit that acknowledges that Jesus Christ has come in the flesh is from God, but every spirit that does not acknowledge Jesus is not from God" (1 John 4:1–3; see 2 John v. 7). John vehemently opposed the denial of Jesus' full humanity, calling it "the spirit of the antichrist."

Another controversy related to the God-man issue was generated in part by Arius of Alexandria in the early fourth century. Arius said Christ was different from God and was of another substance. The conflict that arose from this led to the important Council of Nicaea in AD 325.

Opposition to Christ's deity was soon followed by a return to the other extreme. Apollinaris of Laodicea held a docetic view of Christ, saying that Christ was not truly human.

Nestorius was another church leader who stumbled over this mystery. He ended up with two persons, saying Jesus as a man was energized by the *logos* of God and effectively denied Jesus' complete deity.

Eutyches in the fifth century arrived at the unusual viewpoint that Christ was neither truly human nor divine, but was a *"tertium quid"* (a "third other").

Following this, the Monophysite group stressed the divine nature in Christ and minimized his human nature to such an extent that his humanity was divested of all but a few human characteristics. That represented another swing back to the docetic (not completely human) view of Christ.

Though representatives of both extremes regarding the God-man continued to persist, beginning in the seventh century, the major christological controversies centered more on Christ's work than his person. The next major group to deny his deity in favor of his humanity were the Socinians in the sixteenth century. Since then, the most common trend in avoiding the God-man mystery has been a simple rejection of the biblical testimony concerning Christ's deity, supported largely by eighteenth- and nineteenth-century philosophy, the evolutionary hypothesis, and higher criticism. The docetic extreme of minimizing Jesus' true humanity was more common in the days of the early church and isn't often found today.

THE NICENE CREED
"I believe ... in one Lord Jesus Christ, ... very God of very God, ... made man."
THE ATHANASIAN CREED
"We confess that our Lord Jesus Christ ... is God and man.... Perfect God and perfect man, ... who, although he is God and man, yet he is not two, but one Christ."

The Nicene Creed (present form from the early fifth century) and the Athanasian Creed (early sixth century) give concise statements about Jesus Christ, the God-man.

OTHER FALSE VIEWS OF CHRIST

Outside of the main lines of church history, many more examples of the two extremes (a denial of Christ's deity or of his humanity) can be found in the beliefs of cults and Eastern religions concerning Jesus Christ. Several of these religions regard Christ as simply another prophet sent by God to help enlighten the people of his day. Along with this goes the claim that other prophets with an even greater message have succeeded Jesus, and people of today should first listen to them (for instance, Muhammad, Baha'u'llah, and—more recently—Sun Myung Moon). Other groups think of Jesus as "divine" in the same pantheistic sense in which all men are divine, thus rejecting Christ's exclusive claims.

Another popular approach, which has been supported by various esoteric and occult teachings, is the separation of Jesus from Christ. This is an old idea that goes back to second- and third-century Monarchianism. Some, like Paul of Samosata, taught that "the Christ" (the divine power) descended upon the man Jesus at his baptism and left him just prior to his crucifixion. This has been extended by some today into the idea that all of us can have this divine power or "Christ consciousness" within us.

All these erroneous teachings concerning the God-man place faith in human reason above God's revelation. Thus, it is imperative for each true believer in Christ to accept by faith all the scriptural data. He must not rationalize or disregard elements that tax his comprehension, or he'll be guilty of subjectively choosing those parts of the Bible he likes and eliminating the rest.

SOME RELATED ISSUES

At this point, it may be helpful to deal specifically with some practical problems and questions related to the God-man mystery. Remember, since these problems are related directly to a true mystery, by definition there can be no really satisfying solutions to them on a human level. They only illustrate the nature and implications of the mystery of the God-man.

One related issue is Christ's preexistence and eternality prior to his incarnation. Many Old and New Testament passages make it clear that Christ existed before he was born of Mary and that there never was a time when Christ was not (Mic. 5:2; John 1:1–2; 8:58).

Christ has always existed without a body apart from time and space as equal with the Father and with the Holy Spirit. He was always the Son of God by eternal generation from the Father.[1]

Yet, while he is the same one who has forever existed, in another way he is different. Before he became man he always possessed a divine nature, but since that time he now possesses a divine-human nature (the word *nature* referring to essential qualities or intrinsic properties). He still subsists as the same person, but he is now a divine-human person.

This concept that there is now a God-man in heaven and that Christ now has a divine-human nature affects the Trinitarian relationship because Christ is part of the Godhead. There's a close relationship between the two mysteries of the God-man and the Trinity. But even though Christ will forever have a body he never possessed in eternity past, God's immutability remains: He has not changed in his essence or in his subsistence (mode of being).

It was God's will or decree from eternity past that Jesus Christ would take on human flesh and human nature in the context of God's space-time creation. This timeless plan provided that Christ would have a divine-human nature while remaining a single personality (see John 1:1–14; 1 John 1:1–3; Phil. 2:6–11). Part of the problem here is the question of what controlled the interaction of these two 100 percent entities.

It wouldn't be accurate to say that "Jesus did this out of his humanity" or "he did that out of his deity." This would divide his personality and imply that the association between Christ's humanity and his deity is mutually exclusive. The real affiliation between the human and the divine in the person of Jesus Christ is an unsolvable mystery, since no one has the intellectual capacities to relate to such a combination.

The concept of God's revelation in Christ, the God-man, was so overwhelming to philosopher Søren Kierkegaard that he called it "the absolute paradox."[2] This was part of the basis for his "leap of faith" into the unknown, into the fact that cannot be a fact. For Kierkegaard, the absolute paradox is a scandal to reason because it simultaneously unites the nonhistorical with the historical in the person of the God-man. Because of this, Kierkegaard believed that faith and reason cannot be harmonized. Most Christian scholars part company with him on this point.

THE PROBLEM OF THE *KENOSIS*

The great passage that describes the *kenosis* (self-emptying) of Jesus Christ is Philippians 2:5–11. The *kenosis* is related directly to Christ's nature as God and man, and verses 6–8 portray what was involved: "Who, being in very nature God, did not consider equality with God something to be grasped, but made himself nothing, taking the very nature of a servant, being made in human likeness. And being found in appearance as a man, he humbled himself and became obedient to death—even death on a cross!"

Some have tried to argue from this passage that Christ surrendered his deity in becoming a man. These verses don't support this view but instead teach that the union of Christ to unglorified humanity was the supreme picture of his extreme humility and condescension based on his love for men.

Also involved in Christ's self-emptying is his voluntary nonuse of some of his attributes, particularly omniscience, omnipresence, and omnipotence. This doesn't mean he surrendered these attributes; he couldn't do so without losing his deity, since these attributes are an essential part of God's nature.

Voluntary nonuse means he personally willed not to exercise them on most occasions while he was on earth. Christ veiled his resplendent glory from his birth to his ascension, but he wasn't divested of this intrinsic glory any more than placing a filter over a floodlight diminishes the brightness of the lamp itself. On at least two occasions this veil was taken away for a short time (the transfiguration and in the garden of Gethsemane). In summary, the Creator of the heavens and the earth humbled himself to become a perfect man.

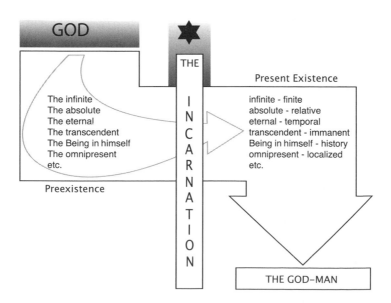

The doctrine of the *kenosis* of Christ raises other questions. How could he have learned anything when he was a child, if he was at the same time the omniscient God? How could Jesus as God learn "obedience from what he suffered" (Heb. 5:8)? The impenetrable answers must lie in the nature of how Christ could voluntarily not use his "omni" attributes for periods of time. Somehow the omniscient Lord Jesus was able to veil his omniscience from himself without diminishing his deity or perfection. As a man, he required preparation before he could begin his public ministry, and it could be said that "Jesus grew in wisdom and stature, and in favor with God and men" (Luke 2:52).

Another question concerns Christ's ability to control his miraculous resources. With respect to his human nature, Jesus needed to mature or "grow" in four basic areas: intellectually ("wisdom"), physically ("stature"), spiritually, and socially ("in favor with God and men")—but from the standpoint of his divine nature, Jesus as God can't mature but is always perfect.

It is difficult to comprehend how the interaction of Christ's dual nature worked so that he always had perfect physical and mental control over his supernatural abilities.

The idea of a human with superhuman endowment has always intrigued the popular mind. Variations on this theme have been developed in science fiction (cyborgs and people of superhuman intelligence); children's comic books, TV shows, and films (especially superheroes like Superman); and the alluring promises of supernatural abilities offered by witchcraft, the occult, and the black arts.

In reality, due to the problem of sin, a person's powers are directly proportional to his potential for wickedness and destruction. For example, if a person like Superman really existed, the world or at least a large proportion of mankind would probably have been destroyed long before he reached maturity by some fit of anger when he was a child. Even if the world did survive his maturation, people everywhere would be gripped by his controlling hand, waiting in dread for his next odious impulse or appetite to become law.

We can thank God that Jesus Christ's limitless abilities were wonderfully controlled and exercised because of his undiminished deity and perfect humanity. Christ was always motivated by love and compassion for men and was incapable of sinning because he could not go against his own nature as God.

Another question that relates to Christ's early childhood and his voluntary nonuse of his omniscience during most of his time on earth concerns his knowledge of his own person and ministry. How much of his destiny did he know, and when did he realize he was the Messiah? Scripture indicates that at least by the age of twelve Jesus was clearly aware of his identity as the Son of God (Luke 2:49). As for his complete awareness of his mission as the substitutionary sacrifice for the sins of the world, the Gospels show Jesus had a clear knowledge of this at least by the time he was baptized by John.

Since the Scriptures are mostly silent about Jesus' life before he began his public ministry, a more definite answer to these questions can't be given. It lies in the mystery of how he could know all things as God and voluntarily choose to limit his knowledge at the same time.

Incidentally, these eighteen to twenty "silent years" in Christ's life from age twelve (Luke 2:41–52) until his baptism by John (Luke 3:1–22) have been seized by representatives from various religions, cults, and the occult in an attempt to diminish Christ's deity and reduce him to a precursor of these false systems.

Some, for instance, have taught that he derived most of his teachings from the Essene community during this time. Others say he spent some of these years in India, where he was initiated into the labyrinths of Hinduism. When evidence for this curious viewpoint is requested, they proudly reply that John the Baptist was Jesus' guru!

Several apocryphal books have attempted to spice up these unknown years by ascribing bizarre miracles to Jesus. This kind of preoccupation with things not revealed in Scripture is misguided, since God has purposely chosen to veil them. The apostle John said specifically, "Jesus did many other things as well. If every one of them were written down, I suppose that even the whole world would not have room for the books that would be written" (John 21:25).

Other enigmatic questions concerning the God-man can be connected with the nature of the virgin birth, such as: At what point before his birth did Jesus become the God-man?

Another passage that has an interesting bearing on the God-man mystery is the description of Christ's work in Colossians: "For by him all things were created ... and in him all things hold together" (1:16–17). Not only did the Lord Jesus cause all things to exist, but he also continues to sustain his entire creation at all times and in all places. If Christ failed to hold creation together for a moment, all things in the heavens and on the earth would undergo atomic dissolution! This is precisely what will happen in the future when God destroys this universe and creates a new and eternal heaven and earth (2 Peter 3:10–13).

There's no way of knowing how Christ is holding the universe together, but it may be related to the inexplicable "strong force" (as physicists term it) that holds the nuclei of all atoms together. The positively charged particles that are packed so closely together in atomic nuclei might be expected to repel each other because they have the same charge, yet they remain compact. If this binding force in all atoms were removed, all matter in the universe would come apart, and all things could be reduced to pure energy.

This passage (Col. 1:16–17) connects with the God-man mystery in that, since Christ had a human body, he physically was composed of atoms and molecules. Christ, therefore, must literally have been holding himself together while on earth. The word translated "hold together" *(synistemi)* can mean "continue, endure, exist, consist, or be composed" in this context. (This is also true of 2 Peter 3:5, where it is also connected with the existence or enduring of the heavens.)

After his resurrection, Christ took on a new body of glorified flesh, a body suitable for a heavenly existence (see 1 Cor. 15:42–51). Jesus now possesses this same body in heaven, and though it relates to the mystery of the resurrection body (see chapter 6), it can still be said that Christ as the self-existent God will forever continue to hold himself together and maintain his consistence.

One final consideration concerning this mystery: How could Christ be temptable and impeccable (incapable of sinning) at the same time? These two facts are suggested in Hebrews: "For we do not have a high priest who is unable to sympathize with our weaknesses, but we have one who has been tempted in every way, just as we are—yet was without sin" (4:15). While this verse does not prove that Christ wasn't able to sin, the Scriptures teach that there was a significant difference between his humanity and ours in that he had no sin nature. While his human nature was peccable, in the totality of his person as the God-man he was impeccable.

Since being temptable and at the same time being impeccable is beyond our grasp, the only thing we can say is that his temptability relates to his complete humanity and his impeccability is connected with his complete deity. Christ could not have sinned on any occasion, for he is God. Yet Christ was "tempted in every way, just as we are." The temptation was very real, for he was fully human.

How Can We Model the God-man?

Christians are supposed to model their lives after Christ. "To this you were called, because Christ suffered for you, leaving you an example, that you should follow in his steps. 'He committed no sin, and no deceit was found in his mouth'" (1 Peter 2:21–22; see also 1 Peter 1:14–16).

How can Christ be our example and model when he was also God? How can we follow in the steps of the One who committed no sin?

To some it seems almost unfair. But Paul says it can be done: "Follow my example, as I follow the example of Christ" (1 Cor. 11:1). Here he is claiming that his life is so Christlike that others can and should imitate it.

How can our lives attain this quality? As it's often said, "The Christian life is not difficult—it's impossible!" The solution is seen in Paul's statement, "I have been crucified with Christ and I no longer live, but Christ lives in me. The life I live in the body, I live by faith in the Son of God, who loved me and gave himself for me" (Gal. 2:20). Paul's life of modeling Christ was possible only insofar as he appropriated the power of the indwelling God.

The Christian life, then, is a divine-human process. It is a supernatural, not a natural, life. God has not told us, "Here are the rules. Good luck!" Instead, all who have received Christ are indwelt by the Father, the Son, and the Holy Spirit (John 14:16–23). Christians are empowered by the eternal Godhead, but we need to allow this power to control and transform our lives by faith.

The God-man's life is, therefore, a valid model for all believers because the living, indwelling God offers divine enablement to all Christians who want it. Paul mentions this divine-human process in the Christian life: "Work out your salvation with fear and trembling, for it is God who works in you to will and to act according to his good purpose" (Phil. 2:12–13). Verse 12 describes the human and verse 13 the divine role in the outworking of the Christian life.

Christ's true humanity is graphically depicted by the author of Hebrews: "During the days of Jesus' life on earth, he offered up prayers and petitions with loud cries and tears to the one who could save him from death, and he was heard because of his reverent submission. Although he was a son, he learned obedience from what he suffered and, once made perfect, he became the source of eternal salvation for all who obey him" (5:7–9). Christ offered up prayers and "learned obedience," and he was empowered by the Holy Spirit and sustained by his heavenly Father. All Christians will do well to follow his example.

A person who is in Christ has the potential to choose not to sin in any given situation. Since the living God indwells him, he can choose to "put on the new self, created to be like God in true righteousness and holiness" (Eph. 4:24).

However, because the flesh (what Paul calls "another law at work in the members of my body" in Rom. 7:23) is still with us, the fact that we can choose not to sin on specific occasions doesn't mean we can become sinlessly perfect in this life. The apostle John makes it clear that until the flesh is removed from believers, we will continue to sin: "If we claim to be without sin, we deceive ourselves and the truth is not in us" (1 John 1:8; see 1:10—2:2). But since we have access to God's supernatural power by grace through faith, Christ's life is still a valid example for all of God's children to follow. "So I say, live by the Spirit, and you will not gratify the desires of the sinful nature" (Gal. 5:16). Jesus walked in the power of the Holy Spirit, and Scripture calls us to do the same.

> I am the light of the world. Whoever follows me will never walk in darkness, but will have the light of life. (John 8:12)
>
> I am the bread of life. He who comes to me will never go hungry, and he who believes in me will never be thirsty. (John 6:35)
>
> Whoever drinks the water I give him will never thirst. Indeed, the water I give him will become in him a spring of water welling up to eternal life. (John 4:14)
>
> Do nothing out of selfish ambition or vain conceit, but in humility consider others better than yourselves. Each of you should look not only to your own interests, but also to the interests of others. (Phil. 2:3–4)

THIRTY YEARS LATER

- It's important to emphasize that this book isn't espousing irrationalism. Human reason, though it is limited and can be distorted by sin, is still part of God's image within us.

- The forces of religious pluralism and syncretism in the last three decades have increased the popular tendency to minimize the uniqueness and deity of Jesus Christ—not only in popular culture, but also among a growing number of theologians.

- My book *Conformed to His Image* (Zondervan, 2001) comprehensively explores and recounts the diverse paths and stages of spiritual growth and becoming like Christ. I see now that the brief words "model [our] lives after Christ" and "follow in his steps" used in this book must be read to embrace the fullness of becoming like Christ in multiple dimensions, such as devotional, disciplined, nurturing, Spirit-filled, and corporate spirituality.

- Even as followers of Christ, we will continue to struggle against the human instinct to oversimplify him or reduce his life and existence to manageable cognitive proportions. Though we can know and love him (1 Peter 1:8) in this life, we can only see him "in a mirror dimly" (1 Cor 13:12 NASB).

- In recent years, people have been widely exposed to a number of distorted and heretical views of Jesus, including the Jesus Seminar, the Gnostic gospels (including the gospels of Thomas, Judas, and Mary Magdalene), a wide variety of TV documentaries and reconstructions, conspiracy literature, and *The Da Vinci Code* (which has been embraced by many as though this page-turner is fact rather than fiction).

Chapter 3

THE TRINITY

Theology, the study of God, appears to many to be too presumptuous and ambitious a project. Even some theologians cut off the branch they're sitting on by denying that any genuine study can be made of God. How can we who are finite speak meaningfully about the infinite? How can the inscrutable and incomprehensible be described in human terms?

Theologian Paul Tillich even went so far as to say that God is beyond existence and beyond supernaturalism. For Tillich, the question of God's existence is out of order, let alone the possibility of knowing specific things about him.[1] This kind of approach, for him, can only lead to negative results—what God is *not*.

As long as we set up our own minds as the standard for truth, we can't attain a real knowledge of God. The problem of knowing God is solved in one word: *revelation*. When God's Word instead of unaided human reasoning becomes the basis for truth, answers are possible.

THE PROBLEM

Because the living God has revealed himself to us, we can make positive and specific statements about him based on this revelation. We can confidently describe many of his attributes, such as holiness, justice, love, and immutability. Though we'll never know all there is to know about God, we can be satisfied that the things he has told us about himself in the Bible are true. Moreover, those who have trusted in Christ know God in a personal as well as an intellectual way.

Nevertheless, Christians recognize many things about God are mysterious, incomprehensible, and superrational. God in his existence as the three-in-one is beyond the limits of human comprehension.

The Scriptures reveal not only the complete unity of the Godhead but also the equally complete distinctiveness of the three persons who make up the Godhead. Through all eternity there is a perfect and absolute unity and diversity because the Godhead is one and three.

The term *Trinity* is generally used to describe the Godhead. The *tri* emphasizes God's threeness and the *ity* emphasizes his unity. He is a "Triunity." Although the term *Trinity* isn't found in Scripture, this doesn't prohibit its usefulness in the study of God's revealed nature.

SCRIPTURAL PROOF FOR THE TRINITY

We can demonstrate the Trinity of God by giving biblical evidence first for his unity, then for his threeness, and finally look at some verses that combine these two truths.

It's clear from both the Old and New Testaments that there is but one God, not three. "You shall have no other gods before me" (Ex. 20:3; Deut. 5:7) is the first of the Ten Commandments. One of the clearest and best known statements of God's unity is, "Hear, O Israel: The LORD our God, the LORD is one" (Deut. 6:4).

Isaiah writes, "Remember the former things, those of long ago; I am God, and there is no other; I am God, and there is none like me" (46:9; see also Deut. 32:39). "Before me no god was formed, nor will there be one after me" (Isa. 43:10).

New Testament passages such as 1 Corinthians 8:4–6; Ephesians 4:4–6; and James 2:19 also reveal the fact that "there is no God but one" (1 Cor. 8:4).

Nevertheless, God is also three. Even the Hebrew Bible implies that the unity of God is a corporate unity. God revealed himself to man in a progressive way over the approximately 1,500 years during which the Bible was written. The Old Testament often implies what the New Testament declares explicitly.

Several important hints in the Old Testament foreshadow the New Testament revelation of God's three-in-oneness. One of these is the name *Elohim*, which is translated *God,* but is plural in form.

God also often uses the plural pronoun to describe himself: "Then God said, 'Let us make man in our image, in our likeness'" (Gen. 1:26; also compare Gen. 3:22; 11:7; Isa. 6:8).

Another strong hint for the Trinity relates to the person of the Messiah. Isaiah reveals him to be equal with God, calling him the "Mighty God, Everlasting Father, Prince of Peace" (9:6). The Messiah is also coeternal with God according to Micah 5:2.

An example of one who is separate from yet identical with God is the angel of the Lord described in Genesis 22:15–16.[2] This combination of distinctness and identity is also obvious in Isaiah 48:16. In this passage, the Lord is the speaker, yet he refers to the two other persons of the Godhead by saying, "And now the Sovereign LORD God has sent me, with his Spirit."

But the case for God's threeness is far stronger in the New Testament. There it can be shown unequivocally that the Father is God, the Son is God, and the Holy Spirit is God. The New Testament also teaches that these three names are not synonymous, but speak of three distinct and equal persons.

The New Testament leaves no doubt that the Father is God. God is called the Father by Peter (1 Peter 1:2), John (John 6:27), and Paul (Eph. 4:6).

BIBLICAL BASIS FOR THE DOCTRINE OF THE TRINITY
"The LORD our God is one LORD" (Deut. 6:4 KJV)

The BEING of GOD who/what he is (attributes)	FATHER	SON	HOLY SPIRIT
DEITY	Rev. 21:3–7	John 1:1	Acts 5:3–4
SELF-EXISTENCE	Ex. 3:14–15	John 8:58	Gen. 1:2
ETERNITY	Ps. 90:2	John 17:5	Heb. 9:14
OMNISCIENCE	Jer. 17:10	Matt. 9:4	1 Cor. 2:11
OMNIPRESENCE	Jer. 23:24	Matt. 28:20	Ps. 139:7
OMNIPOTENCE	Ps. 62:11	Heb. 1:3	Job 33:4
GOODNESS	Rom. 2:4	Eph. 5:25	Neh. 9:20
HOLINESS	Lev. 11:44	Acts 3:14	John 14:26
ABSOLUTE TRUTHFULNESS	John 7:28	Rev. 3:7	1 John 5:6

The WORKS of GOD What he has done and is doing			
CREATION	Ps. 102:25	Col. 1:16	Gen. 1:2
INSPIRATION	2 Tim. 3:16	1 Peter 1:10–11	2 Peter 1:21
BIRTH OF CHRIST	Gal. 4:4	Heb. 10:5	Luke 1:35
SALVATION OF BELIEVERS	John 1:13	John 1:12	John 3:5–8
INDWELLING OF BELIEVERS	Eph. 4:6	Col. 1:27	1 Cor. 6:19
PROTECTION OF BELIEVERS	John 10:29	John 10:28	Eph. 4:30
PRESENCE FOR WITNESSING	2 Cor. 3:5–6	1 Tim. 1:12	Acts 20:28

Jesus Christ is also God. We considered the biblical evidence for this fact in the previous chapter. His deity is proved by the divine names given him, by his works that only God could do, by his divine attributes (eternality, John 17:5; omnipresence, Matt. 28:20; omnipotence, Heb. 1:3; omniscience, Matt. 9:4), and by explicit statements of his deity (John 1:1; 20:28; Titus 2:13).

The Holy Spirit is God. One of the clearest attestations of this fact is found in Acts 5:3–4, where a lie to the Holy Spirit in verse 3 is equated with a lie to God in verse 4. The deity of the Holy Spirit can also be seen in the divine names used for him (for example, "the Spirit of our God," 1 Cor. 6:11), in his attributes of deity (omnipresence, Ps. 139:7; omnipotence, Job 33:4; omniscience, 1 Cor. 2:10–12), and in his divine works (Gen. 1:2; Luke 1:35; John 3:5–6; 16:8; Rom. 8:26; 2 Peter 1:21).

Thus, the Scriptures teach that God is one and three. A few passages in the New Testament speak of *all three* members of the Godhead as distinct persons. One is Matthew 3:16–17: Jesus is being baptized, the Spirit of God descends upon him as a dove, and the Father speaks from heaven.

There's also the threefold benediction at the end of 2 Corinthians that puts the three persons of God on an equal plane: "May the grace of the Lord Jesus

Christ, and the love of God, and the fellowship of the Holy Spirit be with you all" (13:14).

The verse that seems to best capture the Trinity's balance is Matthew 28:19: "… baptizing them in the name of the Father and of the Son and of the Holy Spirit." Notice the word *name* is singular, indicating the Godhead's unity. At the same time, God's threeness is also indicated by the list of the three persons.

TOWARD A DEFINITION

Here, as in other areas of theology, the Bible does not give us a formal definition. However, it does provide all the essential elements since it speaks of the distinctions within the unified Godhead and tells how the three persons are related.

One of the most satisfactory definitions has been given by Warfield: "There is one only and true God, but in the unity of the Godhead there are three coeternal and coequal persons, the same in substance but distinct in subsistence."[3] The word *substance* speaks of God's essential nature or being, and *subsistence* describes his mode or quality of existence.

However, as good as this definition is, it still falls short of capturing the mystery of the Trinity. For instance, the word *persons* is somewhat misleading because it implies three separate rational and moral individuals. "But in the being of God there are not three individuals, but only three personal self-distinctions within the one divine essence."[4]

The intellect, emotions, and will of the three-in-one God are manifested as much in his oneness as they are in his threeness. The Father, Son, and Holy Spirit are distinct in their personhoods, yet they act and exist as a unit.

Perhaps we should speak of the "three unipersons" of the Godhead to capture the idea that while there are three personal distinctions, they are nevertheless one God.

So there is an ultimate unity within diversity and an ultimate diversity within unity. God has always been the three-in-one, since all three of him always existed. The existence of the Son and of the Holy Spirit is a derivative existence. It is an absolute and nonantecedent; they don't derive their being from the Father. The living God is the absolute one and three. He is contained within himself and exists because of himself.

In formulating a picture of the Trinity, we should also note that while the three are equally divine and eternal, there is nevertheless a strong element of subordination. This subordination isn't intrinsic (since no member is inferior to another) but relational. The Scriptures indicate an order of priority in how God operates and reveals himself.

The Father is especially active as the Originator, Creator, and Sustainer of the universe. Yet the Father's creation is through the Son and by the Holy Spirit. Similarly, while revelation and redemption are most closely linked with the person and work of Jesus, they are from the Father, through the Son, by the Holy Spirit. The same may be said of the Holy Spirit's special ministries.[5]

No Clear Solutions

If these attempts at defining and describing the Trinity leave you befuddled, perhaps the following illustrations will help a bit. But remember, mysteries are beyond human comprehension, so the Trinity isn't going to become completely understandable. You are still going to be left with the mystery that God is one and three. God's Word simply requires us to accept the fact that while the Father, Son, and Holy Spirit are equally, ultimately, and exhaustively God, they are nevertheless distinct from one another.

The figure below is commonly used to concisely visualize the truth about the triune Godhead. Each person is God; each person is also distinct, but God is nevertheless only one God.

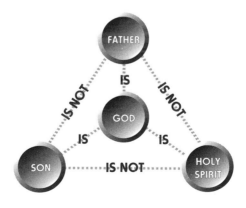

ILLUSTRATIONS HELP, BUT THEY BREAK DOWN

There have been many attempts to illustrate the triune Godhead's nature from creation and from human experience. It is true that God has revealed things about himself in nature (Rom. 1:20). It is also true that man is still in God's image, though fallen. Nevertheless, illustrations from creation and from man's nature can never really capture all the Bible teaches about the Trinity. They can't capture the biblical concept that each of the three is *completely* the infinite One.

On the other hand, there are many "three-in-one" parallels that help in visualizing some aspects of the Trinity. Henry Morris, for instance, describes the physical universe as a "trinity of trinities."[5] Here, the main trinity consists of space, mass-energy (matter), and time. Each of these elements is further divided into another trinity.

THE UNIVERSE

3 DIMENSIONS

SPACE	MATTER	TIME
Length	Energy	Past
Width	Motion	Present
Height	Phenomena	Future

Concerning this space-matter-time universe, Morris writes:

> Space is the invisible, omnipresent background, manifest sensibly everywhere and always in mass-energy, interpreted and experienced in time. The analogy is evident when one substitutes in the foregoing sentence, the words "Father," "Son," and "Spirit," for "space," "mass-energy," and "time," respectively.[6]

Another "three-in-one" illustration is water (H_2O). Water retains its chemical identity whether in the solid, gaseous, or liquid state. Given the proper temperature and pressure, there's also a *triple point* for H_2O. This is a condition under which ice, steam, and liquid water can coexist in equilibrium. The three phases are all H_2O, but they're distinct from one another.

Many actions can also be broken down into three basics: source, manifestation, and meaning (or cause, event, consequence). Two of these are *moral actions* (motive, act, consequences) and *seeing* (the object seen, the act of vision, the mental interpretation).

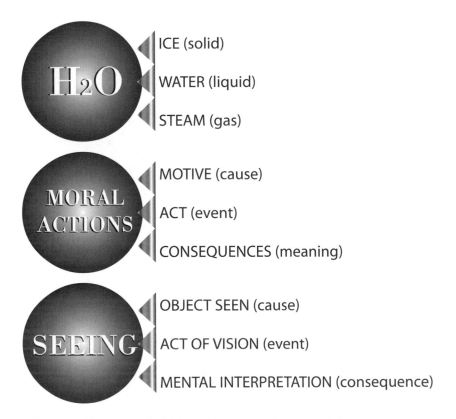

ICE (solid)

WATER (liquid)

STEAM (gas)

MOTIVE (cause)

ACT (event)

CONSEQUENCES (meaning)

OBJECT SEEN (cause)

ACT OF VISION (event)

MENTAL INTERPRETATION (consequence)

Three more illustrations of trinities within nature and human activity.

The idea of three-in-one isn't foreign to human experience since nature appears to have many "trinities." These may be vague shadows of God's ultimate triunity. Though the doctrine of the triune Godhead is far more enigmatic than any of these illustrations, it should be clear that it is not a primitive, foolish, or irrational doctrine. Instead, it is the subtle and profound product of a higher rationality and being.

THE THREE CHOICES

As in the case of the God-man mystery, there are three basic responses a person can make to the biblical idea of the Trinity. First, he can ignore or reject it as incompatible with human reason. Second, he can attempt to reduce it to human level by gravitating toward either extreme (God is one, God is three). Third, he can accept it completely by holding both concepts in a proper balance. In this case, he accepts by faith all of the data of God's Word as true even though it sometimes goes beyond his own understanding.

The one who responds to this mystery in either the first way or the second way has literally assumed the place of God by making his own mind the ultimate criterion for truth. For him, the Bible is true only insofar as he understands it. Those things that seem reasonable are true, and whatever he cannot comprehend must be denied.

THE TWO EXTREMES

In an effort to water down the doctrine of the triune God, many have fallen into error. One such error is Unitarianism, which regards God as only one person. Since, for most, this person is God the Father, Jesus Christ and the Holy Spirit are stripped of their genuine deity. Jesus is reduced to a mere man ("the humble teacher from Nazareth"), and the Holy Spirit is turned into an impersonal force or fluid that emanates from God. The Unitarian Universalist Association is an example of this extreme.

Jehovah's Witnesses are essentially unitarian because they deny Christ's deity and view the Holy Spirit as an impersonal force.[7] This new form of Arianism repudiates the Trinity because it deems it unreasonable.

The second extreme is tritheism. This is a variation of polytheism because the Father, Son, and Holy Spirit are regarded as three separate Gods. Sometimes this is carried a step further into the idea that there are many different gods, some perhaps associated with other worlds or realms. Mormonism

is an example of tritheism, for it speaks of the Father, the Son, and the Holy
Spirit as three distinct Gods.[8]

The only way to avoid these extremes is to accept all the biblical facts in a
balanced way. The Trinity can't be comprehended by the human mind because
it's superrational. Nevertheless, when anyone places his faith in God and the
truth of his Word, he finds a satisfaction in this and other difficult areas of
revealed truth. There's no need for a continual struggle.

IMPLICATIONS OF THE TRINITY MYSTERY

The nature of the triune Godhead has many practical implications for
Christians. The Trinity provides solutions for some of the dilemmas that have
plagued people for centuries and also relates directly to the critical issues of revelation, prayer, redemption, and fellowship.

1.   *Mysteries are related to one another.* The Trinity and God-man
     mysteries are so closely connected that, as mentioned above, an
     error concerning one leads to an error concerning the other. The
     fact that God the Son became an incarnated man without losing
     his deity profoundly affects the Trinity.

Other doctrines, such as God's decree, the Son's eternal generation, and
the Holy Spirit's procession, are also affiliated with the nature of the Trinity, as
are the mysteries concerning immanence versus transcendence, omnipresence
versus localization, time, the resurrection body, and divine sovereignty versus
human responsibility. Because all things owe their existence to the One who
"calls things that are not as though they were" (Rom. 4:17), we might expect
all these things to be interrelated. "For from him and through him and to him
are all things" (Rom. 11:36).

2.   *The Trinity mystery is an absolute for unity and diversity.* Within
     the Godhead, neither unity nor diversity is more fundamental.
     God himself is the eternal one and three. Thus, the biblical reve-
     lation of the triune God contains the answer to the ancient
     philosophical problem of the one and the many.

The question that men have been unable to answer apart from the Scriptures is, "What gives meaning to the particulars in the universe?" The Bible tells us that because God is eternally one and three, he is the Absolute who unifies and gives meaning to the infinite variety of the created universe. The universe isn't a chaotic product of time and chance. Instead, it's orderly, harmonious, and systematic. God's own diversity is reflected in the diversity of life in creation.

The God of the Bible is the answer to the problem of the absolutes and the universals. Apart from him nothing in the universe would have any real significance. Everything would be relative to everything else in an existence that has no ultimate meaning.

3. *Uniqueness of the Trinity.* The biblical doctrine of the infinite, personal, triune Godhead is unique. Many, however, don't want to accept this, thinking that other religions also have their "trinities." This is usually part of a syncretistic effort to support the notion that all religions are variations of the same thing.

Representatives of this view often point to a trinity of gods in Hinduism known as *Trimurti.* The first god is "the Creator" (Brahma), the second is "the Preserver" (Vishnu), and the third is "the Destroyer" (Shiva). But the major similarity this triad of gods has to the biblical Trinity is the element of threeness.[9] Otherwise, they're quite different.

The same can be said of other triads of gods—for instance, the Egyptian gods Osiris, Isis, and Horus. They are simply three gods that are related. In both Hinduism and the Egyptian pantheon there are many other gods as well. The God of the Bible remains completely unique as the infinite and personal Creator who eternally subsists as the three-in-one.

4. *Redemption and the triune God.* In the Scriptures, God reveals his plan of bringing salvation to men. This entire plan of redemption hinges on the triune Godhead's nature, for the two doctrines stand or fall together. Apart from the Trinity it's inconceivable that the one true God could become a true man, be put to death, and raise himself from the dead.

All three members of the Godhead play critical roles in making our redemption from sin possible. The Father's love prompted him to send his only begotten Son into the world so we might live through him (see 1 John 4:9–10). Christ's love for sinners and his obedience to his Father's righteous will led him to die as our substitute. And the Holy Spirit's loving ministry applies the benefits of Jesus' blood to all who want God's free gift of eternal life.

It follows that those who deny the Trinity must also have a poor view of Jesus Christ, the Holy Spirit, and the nature of salvation.

> 5.   *The ultimate fellowship.* The fact that God is a perfect Trinity means that in him exists all the fullness of being, life, and fellowship. God is living love, self-conscious and dynamic.

Love is impossible without a lover and a beloved. Within the triune Godhead there is a perfect interrelationship of love, lover, and beloved. God can indeed rejoice in himself.

This mutual intimacy within the Godhead is clearly seen in Christ's High Priestly Prayer: "And now, Father, glorify me in your presence with the glory I had with you before the world began.… You loved me before the creation of the world" (John 17:5, 24).

Because God has perfect fellowship and love within his own being, absolutes for fellowship and love exist. And because God created us in his image, we can have true fellowship with God and with one another. God's love for us makes all this possible: "I have given them the glory that you gave me, that they may be one as we are one: I in them and you in me. May they be brought to complete unity to let the world know that you sent me and have loved them even as you have loved me" (John 17:22–23).

Fellowship and love, then, are based completely on the fact that God is a triunity.

When the church is made complete at the resurrection, it will reflect the personal unity and diversity within the Godhead. Perfect fellowship will exist not only among the members of the body of Christ but also between the body of Christ and the living God. The fellowship that we can now enjoy with God and other men is a pale reflection of what God holds in store for those who know Jesus Christ.

6.   *Revelation, prayer, and the Trinity.* God's revelation of himself to
      man is also based on the nature of the Trinity. "As God can, in
      an absolute sense, communicate himself inward in an act of self-
      revelation among the three persons, so he is able, in a relative
      sense, to impart himself outward in revelation and communica-
      tion to his creation."[10]

Even the way we approach God in prayer is dependent on the Trinity. In
prayer, the Holy Spirit intercedes for us, for we do not know how to pray as
we should (Rom. 8:26). The Father is the one to whom we pray, but we must
pray in the name of the Son (see John 16:23–24).

Though we cannot comprehend the biblical doctrine of the Trinity, the
things God has chosen to reveal about his three-in-one nature are extremely
important. The doctrine of the Trinity connects closely with other important
doctrines, including the work of redemption, the God-man, and revelation.
This unique biblical teaching invades everything we know about love, fellowship, prayer, and worship.

> Praise be to the God and Father of our Lord Jesus Christ! In his great
> mercy he has given us new birth into a living hope through the res-
> urrection of Jesus Christ from the dead, and into an inheritance that
> can never perish, spoil or fade—kept in heaven for you, who
> through faith are shielded by God's power until the coming of salva-
> tion that is ready to be revealed in the last time. (1 Peter 1:3–5)

> May the grace of the Lord Jesus Christ, and the love of God, and the
> fellowship of the Holy Spirit be with you all. (2 Cor. 13:14)

THIRTY YEARS LATER

•   Of the three theistic world religions, only biblical Christianity
      teaches the triunity of God. Judaism and Islam teach the unity of
      God but deny that he is a tri-personal being. This is profoundly
      significant, since love can't exist if there's only one person. There
      must be an *I* and a *Thou*, but if God is only an *I*, the result would

be cosmic narcissism. Love requires a lover, a beloved, and the love that flows between them. Augustine related this to the Father, the Son, and the Holy Spirit. This is the ontological basis for interpersonal love, communion, and communication.

- It's good to relate to each of the divine persons in our prayer and meditation rather than limiting ourselves to one. It is also good to relate to the three as one God. This process will stretch our minds and keep us from getting into a cognitive rut in our approach to the mystery we call God.

- Each member of the Trinity is essential for the existence and nature of the other two; God is only complete if expressed in three persons.

- While there have been advancements in the past thirty years related to the space-matter-time illustration I used, the principles still apply.

Chapter 4

DIVINE SOVEREIGNTY VERSUS HUMAN RESPONSIBILITY

(Salvation)

Mysteries are forced upon us by the facts of God's Word; we are not inventing them ourselves. Since his written revelation teaches concepts that appear to be mutually exclusive, we must realize that with God both truths are friends, not enemies. In God's higher rationality, things that we think must be either-or can in reality be both-and.

Thus, *when the biblical facts warrant them,* we can embrace incomprehensibles in the Bible and relate them to God's omniscience and omnipotence. There's no need to abandon rationality for nonsense as the White Queen does in Lewis Carroll's *Through the Looking Glass:*

> "I can't believe *that!*" said Alice.
>
> "Can't you?" the Queen said in a pitying tone. "Try again: draw a long breath, and shut your eyes."
>
> Alice laughed. "There's no use trying," she said, "one *can't* believe impossible things."
>
> "I dare say you haven't had much practice," said the Queen. "When I was your age, I always did it for half-an-hour a day. Why, sometimes I've believed as many as six impossible things before breakfast."[1]

Neither do we need to adopt Tertullian's position: "I believe it because it is absurd." Christians should say instead: "I believe it because God says it in the Bible."

THE GENERAL PROBLEM

God has revealed to us in the Bible that he not only created all things but also preplanned everything that would happen in his creation. He knows both everything that has happened and everything that is yet future. He actively decreed every detail of this reality, and he is sovereign over all. But here is where the mystery comes in: Even though God is sovereign, man still has real responsibility and freedom in the choices he makes. These choices are his own responsibility; he can't blame God for them. And they will genuinely affect and modify the rest of his life.

Because this mystery more intimately affects us than most of the others, it's one of the most difficult to accept. When people face it, they tend to overemphasize one truth (God's sovereignty) or the other (human responsibility). This produces a lack of balance.

This mystery manifests itself in different ways. For instance, it relates to the issue of election and faith in the doctrine of salvation, as we will see later in this chapter. It also relates to the problem of how evil could enter the creation without God being responsible for it. We'll examine this age-old problem in chapter 5.

But first we need to demonstrate from the Word of God the truth of the two basic propositions in this mystery. Do the Scriptures really say that man is completely responsible for what he does even though God planned everything that would come to pass?

DIVINE SOVEREIGNTY

God is able to do anything he desires. "I know that you can do all things; no plan of yours can be thwarted" (Job 42:2). "The LORD does whatever pleases him, in the heavens and on the earth, in the seas and all their depths" (Ps. 135:6). The Lord carries out everything exactly as planned.

"Have you not heard? Long ago I ordained it. In days of old I planned it; now I have brought it to pass" (2 Kings 19:25). "God is not a man, that he should lie, nor a son of man, that he should change his mind. Does he speak and then not act? Does he promise and not fulfill?" (Num. 23:19). All that God has preplanned is as good as done. Nothing can change it, for *there is no authority above God.* As he says through Isaiah, "To whom will you compare me? Or who is my equal?" (40:25).

Because of his complete uniqueness and sovereignty, God is able to declare, "I am God, and there is no other; I am God, and there is none like me. I make known the end from the beginning, from ancient times, what is still to come. I say: My purpose will stand, and I will do all that I please" (Isa. 46:9–10; see also Isa. 14:24, 27; 43:13).

God directs the history of the universe along the course of his foreordained plan. This involves his ability to choose individuals and groups for special purposes in this plan. For instance, God chose Jeremiah, John the Baptist, and Paul to have special missions even before they were formed in their mothers' wombs (Jer. 1:5; Luke 1:15; Gal. 1:15).

God also elects individuals for salvation. Christ speaks of those elect (Matt. 24:22, 24, 31; Luke 18:7), and Paul clearly endorses this concept (Rom. 8:29–33; Col. 3:12; 2 Tim. 2:10; Titus 1:1; see also 1 Peter 1:1–2; 2 John v. 1).

Ephesians 1:4–14 is particularly striking. God's election of those who would be saved is pretemporal, "before the creation of the world" (v. 4). This choice was based on God's love and kindness. "In love he predestined us to be adopted as his sons through Jesus Christ, in accordance with his pleasure and will" (v. 5).

God's sovereignty is self-determined, and this fact is emphasized three times (vv. 5, 9, 11). In God's loving purpose, all things have been designed to lead "to the praise of his glory" (vv. 6, 12, 14). It is best that God works in all things, for only in this way will all things ultimately glorify God. This glorification is consistent with God's love and kindness because he alone is worthy of ultimate glorification. (Nevertheless, God will also glorify all believers at the resurrection when he finally conforms us to the image of his Son. But even God's act of glorifying others will bring greater glory to himself.)

God's sovereign purpose extends to all things in his creation and isn't limited by space or time. This plan is so complete that Scripture declares, "The lot is cast into the lap, but its every decision is from the LORD" (Prov. 16:33). Consider the implications of a statement like this! Ultimately there is no *chance* in this universe because even the workings of probability and statistics are controlled by God. There are no real accidents, and God is surprised by nothing.

We've seen that God's eternal plan is all-inclusive, extending even to his election of those who will be saved.[2]

But what about those not elected for salvation? Most theologians would naturally prefer to limit the bounds of God's sovereign plan at this point. The word *preterition* is often used here, meaning that God "passes by" the nonelect.

However, several passages in Scripture seem to support a more active role on God's part. If this is so, *reprobation* may be a more appropriate word than *preterition*.

Romans 9:10–24 is one passage that should be carefully studied. God has mercy on whom he desires and hardens whom he desires—both verbs are active (v. 18). God's choice isn't based on human merit, but on his mercy and inscrutable purposes. But if God hardens some, how can human responsibility be real? How can he blame the nonelect for not doing his will (v. 19)? God answers that *the question is out of order* (v. 20). We know that there is no injustice with God (v. 14), and therefore, as vessels we must trust the Potter. For man this issue is a mystery.

Another passage along this line is 1 Peter 2:8. Speaking of those who reject Jesus Christ, Peter says that "they stumble because they disobey the message—*which is also what they were destined for.*" Scripture also says, "The LORD works out everything for his own ends—even the wicked for a day of disaster" (Prov. 16:4). Other verses also reveal how God hardens hearts (Isa. 6:10; 44:18; John 12:40; Rom. 11:7–8, 25).

HUMAN RESPONSIBILITY

Human responsibility is just as biblical a doctrine as divine sovereignty. For instance, Romans 9 (God's sovereignty) isn't complete without Romans 10 (human responsibility): "As the Scripture says, 'Anyone who trusts in him will never be put to shame.' For there is no difference between Jew and Gentile—the same Lord is Lord of all and richly blesses all who call on him, for, 'Everyone who calls on the name of the Lord will be saved'" (Rom. 10:11–13).

King Saul furnishes a good example of the reality of human responsibility. His disobedience cost him a kingdom that would have been everlasting: "He would have established your kingdom over Israel for all time" (1 Sam. 13:13). God later said of Saul, "I am grieved that I have made Saul king, because he has turned away from me and has not carried out my instructions" (1 Sam. 15:11).

The Bible makes it clear that we are not pawns in the hands of a deterministic and fatalistic universe. Every command in the Old and New Testaments is proof of the reality of human responsibility from God's perspective.

Many passages neatly juxtapose the truths of God's complete sovereignty and man's responsibility. Consider, for instance, the crucifixion. Men were responsible for putting Jesus to death even though he was "handed over to you by God's set purpose and foreknowledge" (Acts 2:23). Those who gathered together against Jesus simply did what God's "power and will had decided beforehand should happen," according to Acts 4:27–28. This mystery also relates directly to Judas Iscariot and his betrayal of Christ: "The Son of Man will go as it has been decreed, but woe to that man who betrays him" (Luke 22:22; see also John 17:12).

God is the divine Potter who has "the right to make out of the same lump of clay some pottery for noble purposes and some for common use" according to his own purpose (Rom. 9:21). Yet this "clay" has a will and is responsible for the choices it freely makes. (Read Jer. 18:1–12 to see how the prophet subtly intertwines both of these concepts.)

God is omniscient. Even when he changes his mind (as in Jer. 18:8–10), it's because he planned to do so from eternity. In his omniscience, he also knew the Jews would not turn back from their sins (indeed, he had even hardened their hearts; Isa. 63:17). Yet his appeal to Judah was no sham (Jer. 18:11); it was a valid offer. Another Old Testament passage that combines the two themes of God's control and man's responsibility is Isaiah 63:15—65:2.

Philippians 2:12–13 is a very practical passage in which we may observe a perfect balance of these two truths. Paul is talking about the outworking of the Christian life. He emphasizes the aspect of human responsibility in this process (v. 12), and he also emphasizes God's sovereign control (v. 13). God is controlling and man is responsible. Neither of these two verses should be quoted without the other because the Bible keeps both truths in perfect balance.

SYNTHESIS OF DIVINE SOVEREIGNTY AND HUMAN RESPONSIBILITY

God is the supreme Ruler over this universe he created. His plan affects every detail of this creation. This plan is eternal, and there never was another plan. Thus, terms like *purpose, foreknowledge, predestination,* and *election* are logically related, and they are equally timeless. (We will discuss this further in chapter 7.)

God's complete control over his creation is based on his omniscience and omnipotence. Since God knows all things actual and possible, his eternal plan is not based upon blind choice. Instead, God has wisely chosen a plan in which all details will finally work together to bring about the greatest good (the glorification of God). Since God is the absolute of truth, goodness, and love, his plan is a reflection of his own being and nature.

Not only has God chosen the best possible plan; he also has the power and authority to bring it about (omnipotence). When God promises to do something, there's no question it will be done. This is why every biblical prophecy will be perfectly fulfilled.

Nevertheless, God carries out his all-inclusive plan by various means. God may directly intervene, or he may achieve his purpose by an indirect agency (e.g., the laws of nature). He may even fulfill his plan by taking his hands off in a given situation (the phrase "God gave them over" appears three times in Rom. 1:24–28). But God is in control regardless of what means he chooses to use.

The Bible makes it clear that God's work in predestination and election is loving (Eph. 1:4–5; 1 John 4:7), wise (Rom. 11:33; 16:27), and just (Gen. 18:25; Rom. 3:4–6). "The LORD is righteous in all his ways and loving toward all he has made" (Ps. 145:17).

In some inexplicable way, God has seen fit to incorporate human freedom and responsibility into his all-inclusive plan. Even though the Lord is in sovereign control of the details in his creation, he never forces any man to do anything against his will. The fact that he judges sin means he isn't responsible for the commission of the sins he judges. When a person sins, it is because he has freely chosen to do so. Similarly, when someone is confronted with the terms of the gospel, he can freely choose to accept or reject Christ's offer of forgiveness. Because it's free choice, he will be held responsible for the decision he makes (see John 12:48).

In my view, personal and moral responsibility requires free will. While I disagree with those who say that our wills are in total bondage, I am not implying in my use of the terms "freedom" and "free will" that humans are autonomous. We don't control the fundamental realities of our lives (e.g., our time on earth and our abilities), yet our choices are ours.

In biblical terms, this whole mystery can be summed up by saying that God is both King and Judge. "Scripture teaches that, as King, he orders and controls all things, human action among them, in accordance with his own eternal purpose. Scripture also teaches that, as Judge, he holds every man responsible for the choices he makes and the courses of action he pursues."[3]

Finally, *God's plan is not always the same as his desires.* Although his plan controls what men will be, the product often is not what he desires. This is partly because God has chosen to allow human will to operate. For instance, God "wants all men to be saved and to come to a knowledge of the truth" (1 Tim. 2:4; see also 2 Peter 3:9). Yet he has not elected all men ("those who were chosen obtained it, and the rest were hardened," Rom. 11:7 NASB).

Thus, God's plan and desires are two different aspects of his will. He's revealed his desire (what men *ought* to do), but his plan for what specific men *will* do has been hidden for the most part. This is almost a mystery within a mystery, because there's no way we can conceive of how these two aspects of God's will relate together in his mind.

Illustrations

J. I. Packer captures the essence of this mystery when he writes, "Man is a responsible moral agent, though he is *also* divinely controlled; man is

divinely controlled, though he is *also* a responsible moral agent."[4] Many
have attempted to illustrate the interrelation of these two truths, but
because this is a mystery, their attempts have proved inadequate.

All too often, people try to apply illustrations of foreknowledge to
predestination and election. For instance, they may compare God with a
man standing on top of a mountain, looking down at a road that curves
around the base of the mountain. The man can see into the future because
he knows which cars will pass by one another before they become visible
to each other. But God's plan involves more than foreknowledge.
Foreknowledge is passive, but divine control is active.

Another illustration involves a person engineering a situation in such
a way that it creates a desire in another person to make a certain decision.
Courtship is an example. When a man wants a woman to become his wife,
he designs his courtship in such a way that she will respond with a willing yes when he proposes. He plans the situation and perhaps knows she
will accept his proposal, yet she has a free choice to accept or reject. But
even this illustration breaks down. It implies that when we sin, God
seduced us in that direction. But that simply isn't so (we will discuss this
further in chapter 5).

THE ALTERNATIVES AND EXTREMES

As with other biblical mysteries, three alternatives are possible. One can
accept the mystery, reject it as untrue, or rationalize it. To rationalize it,
one must overemphasize one truth and minimize the other, and this leads
to the two extremes.

The correct approach is to learn to live with the mystery by accepting
both truths involved and holding them in tension because of the authority of God's Word. This means the principles should be regarded as
apparent contradictions and not ultimate contradictions. God's revelation
in the Bible is always self-consistent. The only problem is that human
understanding is sometimes deficient. If we could raise our thoughts to
the level of God's thoughts, there would be no mysteries.

But because so many people refuse to let God be wiser than men, they
insist on rationalizing the principles of the divine sovereignty/human

responsibility mystery. Some are exclusively concerned with the former, others with the latter. Either error can lead to very practical problems. Those hung up on human responsibility may overemphasize methods and develop guilt feelings about not witnessing to everyone they meet. Their counterparts may minimize missions and evangelism, saying, "Why bother? The elect are going to get saved anyway."

Prayer also depends on balancing both principles. If God is not sovereign, there's no point in praying, because he's unable to answer most prayers. And if men have no responsibility, then there's no point in praying because nothing we ask or do will affect God's plan in the least.

From a practical standpoint, it seems more objectionable for a Christian to overemphasize the divine sovereignty and minimize human responsibility than vice versa. Since human responsibility relates to *our role*, we need to attend to it. God will take care of his own sovereignty! Yet both errors are harmful, and neither should be embraced.

Some confuse divine sovereignty with fatalism. Christianity isn't fatalistic, however, because it teaches that human responsibility is just as real as divine sovereignty. Furthermore, what is behind fatalism (fate) isn't what is behind divine sovereignty (a living, wise, sinless God).

Another objection that keeps people from accepting this mystery is the problem of evil. Many feel that it is an insult to our intelligence to assert that all things occur for the best as the result of a human providence. If God is sovereign, isn't he the author of the evil all about us? This objection is important, and we'll deal with it in the next chapter.

It comes as no surprise that this mystery has precipitated heated controversies and extreme viewpoints throughout church history. One notable example was Augustine's controversy with the Pelagians. Pelagianism emphasized human freedom to the exclusion of divine sovereignty, and this led to a concept of self-salvation without the need of divine grace.

In recent centuries, the two extreme viewpoints have been ultra-Calvinism (divine sovereignty carried to pure determinism) and certain extreme forms of Arminianism (human responsibility overemphasized).

As mentioned, people often have more problems with this mystery than with others because it's closer to where we live. But we should remember that it's really no more mysterious than the God-man or the Trinity mystery, which Christians are more likely to accept.

EMPHASES OF HISTORIC ARMINIANISM AND CALVINISM

ARMINIANISM Man's Responsibility in Salvation	CALVINISM God's Sovereignty in Salvation
1. Man is a sinner but able to do good and to respond to God.	1. Total Depravity—Man is unable of himself to respond to God.
2. God elects on the basis of forseen faith.	2. Unconditional Atonement—God elects according to his own good pleasure.
3. Christ died for all men.	3. Limited Election—Christ died for the elect only.
4. Man can, because of stubborness and rebellion, resist God's call to salvation.	4. Irresistible Grace—The elect are irresistibly drawn to Christ.
5. The believer may, through persistent sin, fall from grace and be lost.	5. Perseverance of the Saints—The elect can never perish; they will surely persevere.

THE SPECIFIC PROBLEM OF SALVATION

The general divine sovereignty/human responsibility mystery can be applied in a specific way to the nature of salvation. From the standpoint of God's sovereignty, a person is saved because he is elected by God (chosen for salvation). But from the standpoint of our responsible freedom, a person is elected because he receives Christ.

The first truth finds support in a number of biblical passages. For instance, the apostle Paul writes of the power of God "who has saved us and called us to a holy life—not because of anything we have done but because of his own purpose and grace. This grace was given us in Christ Jesus before the beginning of time" (2 Tim. 1:9).

Paul also wrote, "For those God foreknew he also predestined to be conformed to the likeness of his Son, that he might be the firstborn among many brothers. And those he predestined, he also called; those he called, he also justified; those he justified, he also glorified" (Rom. 8:29–30).[5]

It is clear that in his sovereign grace, God took the initiative.

> We're not to think of Jesus Christ as a Third Party
> wrestling salvation for us from a God unwilling to save. No.
> The initiative was with God himself. "God was in Christ recon-
> ciling the world unto himself." Precisely *how* he can have been
> in Christ while he made Christ to be sin for us, I cannot
> explain, but the same apostle states both truths in the same
> paragraph. And we must accept this paradox along with the
> equally baffling paradox that Jesus of Nazareth was both God
> and Man, and yet one Person. If there was a paradox in his
> person, it is not surprising that we find one in his work as
> well.[6]

Because God is sovereign in salvation, none of us can say that we saved our-selves; this is God's work (see Eph. 2:8–9; Titus 3:5).

Nevertheless, the second truth still holds; we are elected because we receive Christ (remember we're speaking of election as an eternal or time-less event). No one can be saved without willingly trusting in Christ for the forgiveness of sins.

> "Sirs, what must I do to be saved?" They replied, "Believe in the
> Lord Jesus, and you will be saved." (Acts 16:30–31)

> Whoever believes in the Son has eternal life, but whoever rejects
> the Son will not see life, for God's wrath remains on him. (John
> 3:36)

The words *believe* and *faith* are active, not passive, terms in the Bible. Believing in Christ is equivalent to receiving him: "Yet to all who received him, to those who believed in his name, he gave the right to become chil-dren of God" (John 1:12).[7]

The two truths of this mystery (one believes because he is elect, and he is elect because he believes) are sometimes found side by side in the same passage. John 6 is an example. Divine sovereignty is emphasized in verses 37, 44, and 65: "No one can come to me unless the Father who sent me draws him" (v. 44). Human responsibility is emphasized in verses 29,

35, 40, and 47: "For my Father's will is that everyone who looks to the Son and believes in him shall have eternal life" (v. 40).

Thus the biblical doctrine of salvation perfectly combines divine sovereignty and human responsibility. God must call and men must respond willingly. This is a unique picture, for only in Christianity is God declared to be the initiator and author of salvation. The only thing we can do is respond by receiving Christ's free offer.

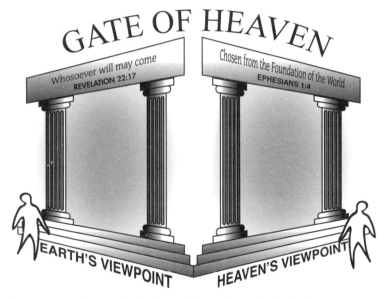

A person standing outside the "gate of heaven" sees the inscription "Whosoever will may come." Passing through and looking back he sees written on the other side, "Chosen from the foundation of the world."

Because of God's sovereignty in salvation, everyone who has trusted Christ for the forgiveness of sins can have assurance of salvation. This certainty comes from the fact that salvation is neither obtained nor maintained by human effort. Since no one deserves it or earns it, eternal life must come by grace through faith. Nevertheless, God will never force anyone to believe in his Son. Free will is still a reality, and all of us are responsible for accepting or rejecting the revelation we've received. As wonderful as the gift of salvation is, if God forced it upon everyone, he would eliminate human freedom.

The Special Case of History

History itself is completely bound up in the divine sovereignty/human responsibility mystery. Because of it the Christian view of history is unique, since it allows for both determinism and free will. "Both apply, but always in such a way that the evil of history is man's work and the good of history, God's."[8] History itself is both a divine product and a human product.

From the divine perspective, "History is not just what happens, but what the living God does."[9] God's relation to history is more than a sequence of interventions; he is always active in usual and unusual ways. God is active in the affairs of all nations and men to bring about his sovereign purpose (see Ps. 33:10–11; Isa. 10:5–15; Dan. 2:21; 4:17; Hab. 1:6).

History, therefore, has a clear goal, and it is moving toward a definite consummation in the second coming and glorious reign of Jesus Christ. Yet at the same time, God has seen fit to give us genuine freedom of choice.

The biblical picture of history offers two crucial elements: the goal of the historical process and the reality of free will. No historian who works from an unbiblical base can logically arrive at either of these elements. Without a revelation from the God who created history, no one could uncover its goal. We are all minute parts of the process, and it would be presumptuous for any part to think he could step out of the process and objectively comprehend the whole.

Neither can the secular historian avoid the problem of determinism. Apart from a personal God, man is left with a deterministic universe driven by forces and laws beyond his control. Only the Bible offers a genuine purpose for history without sacrificing human freedom.

Some Practical Implications of This Mystery

The divine sovereignty/human responsibility mystery has implications for almost every aspect of the Christian life.

1. *Evangelism.* The fact that God sovereignly elects those who will be saved in no way eliminates the Christian's responsibility to share the gospel with those who don't know Christ. God has told us to pray for and witness to non-Christians. It's not our business

to guess who are elected, and they aren't walking around with special signs.

A realization that God is on the throne can give us a confidence in evangelism and should make us bold, patient, and prayerful. Our job is simply to build friendships with unbelievers, share the gospel with them, and pray for them. The results must be entrusted into God's sovereign hands.

> 2.   *Prayer.* If God controls all things, why pray? The answer, of course, is that God commands us to pray, and we're responsible to be obedient to this command. We are also responsible to meet the conditions for answered prayer (some of these conditions are found in John 15:7; 16:23–24; 1 Peter 3:7, 12; 1 John 5:14). Otherwise, our prayers will be hindered.

Though God is sovereign, his children's prayers contribute significantly to the outworking of his program. This doesn't mean that we're pushing buttons or forcing God to answer, for he doesn't grant all requests. Prayer should instead remind a believer of his complete dependence upon God for all things. When great things happen, God is the one who should be glorified, not the person who prayed. So at the same time that God is in control of all things, our prayers can and do profoundly shape reality.

> 3.   *The will of God.* God has a plan for every life, but the details of this plan are carried out by the free choices of each person involved. As we said before, however, God's plan isn't always the same as his desires. *The degree to which God's desires are carried out in his plan for our lives is our responsibility.* God, for instance, desires that we come to love him for who he is and what he's done for us. But we're not robots programmed to say, "Praise you! Praise you!" No one can truly love God (or anyone else) without the power to choose.

The following diagram shows a portion of an individual's life. As time moves in the direction indicated, he makes many choices (represented by dots) that affect other choices. At any given decision point (C), there's a varying range of options or contingencies. For instance, the person may have been accepted at five universities, and he must choose one. The range of options is always limited as indicated by the two lines of *x*'s in the figure. In the case of the prospective student, he has no option to study at a university that did not accept him.

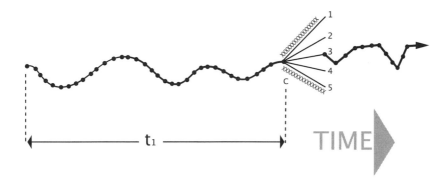

Our person has just come to point C. He can freely choose among five genuine options. Here is where the wonder comes in: *The five contingencies are real, yet whatever is done is God's plan.* This is true for all of us. Because the contingencies are real, we remain responsible for the choices we make.

God sees the whole line at once because he is not limited as we are to the temporal sequence of events (this will be further discussed in chapter 7). Since we can't see our lines of life as God sees them, no one can live his life as though there were a blueprint in front of him. A Christian should instead place his faith in the Lord Jesus Christ for each day's decisions. One can be quite sure about what lies in that past (t1 in the diagram, whether a day or twenty years), but there is a reasonable doubt about what lies ahead.

In general, a non-Christian has fewer options at each decision point because, without the indwelling Holy Spirit, he isn't free to choose those things that would be consistent with God's desires for his life (see Rom. 8:8). Until he allows Christ to liberate him, he is a slave to sin (Rom. 6:17–22; 2 Peter 2:19).

4. *The Christian life.* The Christian's walk with God is a divine-human process. God is always at work in the believer to produce the fruit of righteousness and Christlikeness, but the believer is also responsible for acting. It's not a matter of "let go and let God" on the one hand or of living in the power of the flesh on the other.

Paul communicates this balance clearly: "I have been crucified with Christ and I no longer live, but Christ lives in me. The life I live in the body, I live by faith in the Son of God, who loved me and gave himself for me" (Gal. 2:20; also compare Phil. 2:12–13). God is at work in us, but we're also to *act* in obedience.

5. *Security and comfort.* God is on the throne. He is in complete control of all creation. Even though all things are in constant flux, nothing escapes God's constant notice. "The very hairs of your head are all numbered" (Matt. 10:30). Every time a hair falls out, every time you comb your hair, the Lord takes it into account! Here is Christ's application of this truth: "So don't be afraid" (Matt. 10:31). The fact that God knows you through and through should be a source of great security and comfort. Here is where human responsibility comes in—we respond with trust.

When inexplicable things happen—the untimely death of a loved one, a serious accident—a Christian can find great peace and comfort in the knowledge that a loving God is sovereign in all things.

Next time you're in an airplane, try this exercise. Look down at a city and watch all the tiny cars and houses below. Then meditate on the fact that God intimately knows and cares for all of those people. He is concerned and active in the complex web of their decisions, hopes, and trials.

Each of us is significant because the living God places us in high esteem. "This is how God showed his love among us: He sent his one and only Son into the world that we might live through him" (1 John 4:9).

6. *"Fate" and "luck."* "The lot is cast into the lap, but its every decision is from the LORD" (Prov. 16:33). In view of the overwhelming scriptural evidence for divine sovereignty, terms

like *fate* and *luck* lose their significance. In an ultimate sense, nothing happens by pure chance.

Nevertheless, the biblical doctrine of human responsibility is just as clear, and the lives of all people bear this out. No one can live as though he were a machine programmed by the forces of fate. He must make choices.

7.   *Avoiding responsibility.* We have an ability to contemplate the future and a desire to affect it. The problem is we want to exercise free will, but we do not want the responsibility that goes with it. People try to avoid responsibility in many ways.

One effort has been to set up a random universe in which the causal agents are time and chance. Atheistic evolutionism is an attempt to kick out the owner of the universe. If we don't have to answer to a personal Creator, there's no need to worry about responsibility for our sinful actions and thoughts.

Another effort in some psychiatric schools of thought is the idea that determinism plays an important role. For instance, "Freudian psychoanalysis turns out to be an archaeological expedition back into the past in which a search is made for others on whom to pin the blame for the patients' behavior. The fundamental idea is to find out how others have wronged him."[10] A person's behavior is determined by factors beyond his control (God, religion, parents). But the Bible makes it clear that regardless of the past, no one can blame another for his own bad behavior.

The fatalism of astrology is another deterministic escape hatch. Enthusiasts of astrology desire the power to control their destiny in spite of the fatalism of the system. In a practical sense, the fatalism is useful to the extent that it offers an escape from moral responsibility.

In this last section we've considered only a few of the implications of the divine sovereignty/human responsibility mystery. The biblical truths involved in God's sovereign purpose and control of his universe should lead us to a greater appreciation of God himself. The more we meditate on these things, the more we can picture his loving concern, wisdom, holiness, and greatness.

Show me your ways, O LORD,
teach me your paths;
guide me in your truth and teach me,
for you are God my Savior,
and my hope is in you all day long.
Remember, O LORD, your great mercy and love,
for they are from of old. (Ps. 25:4–6)

My sheep listen to my voice; I know them, and they follow me. I give them eternal life, and they shall never perish; no one can snatch them out of my hand. My Father, who has given them to me, is greater than all; no one can snatch them out of my Father's hand. I and the Father are one. (John 10:27–30)

For I am convinced that neither death nor life, neither angels nor demons, neither the present nor the future, nor any powers, neither height nor depth, nor anything else in all creation, will be able to separate us from the love of God that is in Christ Jesus our Lord. (Rom. 8:38–39)

Thirty Years Later

- People cannot live and act consistently from a deterministic point of view, because experience teaches us every day that we make real choices. We must live as if we have this freedom. At the same time, God knows our past, present, and future actions. We live wisely and choose biblically when we embrace the apparent tension between both these truths.
- In recent years, open theism (also known as free-will theism) has become a growing force among theologians. This teaching denies God's omniscience and timelessness and claims he can't know decisions people will make in the future. On this account, God cannot know all future events, because if he did, there could be no human freedom. This is a mistaken attempt to resolve the central mystery in this chapter that God is able to cause people to make free choices. It also limits God to the dimension of time, which is actually part of his creation.
- Some theologians also minimize God's action in the world and deny or strongly limit his intimate involvement in creation,

preservation, and human history. This growing neodeism necessarily repudiates or reinterprets clear biblical texts to the contrary, such as Job 38—41, most of Psalms, and our Lord's affirmation of God's intimate providential care (Matt. 6:26–34).

- These trends illustrate the continued predominance of Arminianism in recent years, not only among theologians, but also on a popular level. An overemphasis on human freedom, for example, is the underlying fabric of the prosperity gospel and the word-faith movement. The last three decades have seen a growing emphasis on the power to leverage biblical "principles" for personal gain, effectively reducing God to a cosmic vending machine.

- Scripture affirms we can't *contribute* anything to God, since he has no needs or limitations. Nevertheless, we can *participate* in the unfolding of his purposes (e.g., Est. 4:13–14). For example, his purposes in bringing the elect to salvation will be realized whether we participate or not, but he offers us an opportunity to be a very real part of this process that will bear eternal fruit.

Chapter 5

DIVINE SOVEREIGNTY VERSUS HUMAN RESPONSIBILITY

(The Problem of Evil)

T he Bible teaches that "God is light; in him there is no darkness at all" (1 John 1:5). He is the absolute standard of goodness. And as the sovereign Lord, he is both all-knowing and all-powerful.

If these things are true, why is his creation so full of evil? He planned the universe, and he continues to control every detail. Yet the world abounds with destruction and misery. Isn't God the one who's ultimately to blame?

Evil is traditionally divided into two basic types. The first is *natural evil.* There are many evils in the "natural disease-death environment"[1] that are hard to reconcile with the purposes of a loving and omnipotent God. Thousands of lives are lost or ruined because of earthquakes, floods, plagues, and other natural disasters. People all over the world suffer the agonies of slow and cruel diseases and other organic defects. It's only too easy to find examples of situations that show no intelligent purpose.[2] Nature seems to disregard justice and mercy as it indiscriminately attacks the righteous as well as the wicked.

There is also the whole area of animal pain and suffering. In the natural order, most animals and insects maintain their existence by destroying others. It seems to be simply the survival of the fittest. Does God approve of this might-makes-right environment?

The second type of evil is *moral evil.* By far the greatest evil is man's rebellion against God. According to the Scriptures, man's sin (defined as anything contrary to the character of God) has devastating results. But couldn't God foresee that people would disobey him? "If God knew that certain of his creatures were destined to an eternal sentence in hell, we may ask why he created them at all. Is it correct to think of God in some diabolical laboratory dividing people into two groups, rescuing some and rejecting others?"[3]

Moral evil also includes man's cruelty to man. Painful as the physical disease-death environment may be, mental anguish is more fearsome. Totalitarianism, war, greed, jealousy, hatred, and pride cause tremendous anxiety, fear, and insecurity. Sin begets sin in a vicious circle that is constantly spiraling downward.

There's no question that we are directly responsible for the pain and destruction caused by all forms of moral evil. But in a secondary or ultimate sense, isn't God responsible for planning things this way?

Carnell summarizes the basic ingredients of the problem:

> Either God wants to prevent evil, and he cannot do it; or he can do it and doesn't want to; or he neither wishes to nor can do it; or he wishes to and can do it. If he has the desire without the power, he is impotent; if he can, but has not the desire, he has a malice which we cannot attribute to him; if he has neither the power nor the desire, he is both impotent and evil, and consequently not God; if he has the desire and the power, whence then comes evil, or why does he not prevent it?[4]

INADEQUATE SOLUTIONS

The Bible clearly teaches that evil exists though God is omnipotent and good. The question of *how* this can be true is the problem of evil. Many attempts over the years have tried to solve this problem by minimizing God's goodness or omnipotence or by denying the reality of evil. These inadequate solutions have appeared because people are rarely willing to let God's wisdom be greater than theirs. Some may really desire to justify God by defending him, but in their zeal to help they sometimes water down the Bible's truths. Others have no desire to defend God. They indignantly point to evil, attacking the Scriptures with the rhetorical question, "Is *this* your God?"

Here are some of the "solutions" that fall short of solving the problem:

1. *God's goodness is different from man's goodness. God is good in the sense that he exists.* This amounts to redefining the word "good." It's meaningless to call God good if there's little correspondence between what God is and what we call good. This view ultimately denies God's goodness.

2. *All evils are punishments for sin.* This is unsatisfactory for two reasons. First, this would mean God uses punishment unfairly. For instance, the wicked often prosper, while the righteous frequently suffer. The innocent suffer for the crimes of others (e.g., children during wars). "Punishments" are out of proportion to sins committed.

    A second flaw in this solution is it's unbiblical. Christ gave examples of people suffering because of another's moral evil (Luke 13:1–3) and because of natural evil (vv. 4–5). Concerning the latter, the Lord says, "Those eighteen who died when the tower in Siloam fell on them—do you think they were more guilty than all the others living in Jerusalem? I tell you, no! But unless you repent, you too will all perish" (also see John 9:1–3).

3. *God is somehow "beyond" good and evil.* He created both. This is similar to the first solution because it ultimately denies that God is good, at least in the ordinary sense of the word.

4. *The problem of evil is exaggerated.* Even if it is, evil still exists. The quantity of evil has little to do with the problem. C. S. Lewis correctly argues that no individual suffers the composite of human misery (only Christ did this when he was on the cross, bearing the sins of men). This observation may alleviate the problem but doesn't solve it. It's the quality of evil's existence in the universe that we must deal with.

5. *Evil is only an illusion.* This is the solution of pantheists. Evil must not be real if God is all and all is God. Christian Science is probably the best known Western example of this position. This viewpoint forces one to deny the evidence of his senses. But when he does that, what basis does he have left for believing his senses when he reads and hears about the doctrines of Christian Science? Besides, the *illusion* of evil is quite real, and Christian Scientists call this illusion an *evil* that must be fought.

6.　　*God is struggling against evil, but he is not omnipotent.* In this view God is not to blame for evil because he's not powerful enough to overcome it. God is good, but he's fighting a coeternal principle (or god) of evil. This position, which has been promoted widely by Rabbi Harold Kushner in his popular book *When Bad Things Happen to Good People* is known as pluralism, because it holds that there's more than one ultimate reality. This solution of finite theism distorts the Scriptures; diminishes the power, majesty, and glory of God; and removes any assurance that God will ever overcome evil. If God has been unsuccessful after an eternity of struggle, what hope is there for him to overcome evil in another eternity?

THE DIVINE SOVEREIGNTY/HUMAN RESPONSIBILITY ANSWER

We've seen that attempts to solve the problem of evil by denying one or more of its ingredients all lead to a dead end. If God is not omnipotent, he is not in control and there is no hope. If God is not good, there is no point in defending him. And if anyone denies the existence of evil, he should also deny the validity of his senses and thoughts.

Only the Bible offers a solution that explains the origin and future overthrow of evil in a universe created by an omnipotent and completely good God. The solution lies within the divine sovereignty/human responsibility mystery. Even though God is omnipotent and sovereign, he created creatures with *genuine* freedom to make real moral choices. These creatures could and did willfully rebel against God and deserve full blame for the evil that resulted. Though God is sovereign, he did not make any creature sin. Everything that came from his hands was originally perfect and sinless.

There's no question that God knew what would happen when he created beings with free will. He knew that Satan and man would introduce evil into a perfect creation as a result of their willful rebellion against their Creator. The real mystery here is that God incorporated sin and evil in the outworking of his plan without being responsible for its commission.

Failure to believe both truths in this biblical mystery can lead to one of two basic extremes. The first is that God never expected sin to exist in his creation. But God's eternal plan, which included the sacrifice of his Son on behalf of sinful humanity, proves that God preplanned for sin. The second extreme is far more common and is a frequent objection by non-Christians to the biblical picture of reality. This is the view that pins the ultimate responsibility for sin on God, sometimes in an attempt to lighten the burden of man's true moral guilt.

This second extreme overemphasizes divine sovereignty to the virtual exclusion of human responsibility. But does divine sovereignty really make God the author of sin? The answer is that God is the designer of a plan that included sin, but he is *never* responsible for committing the sin. We need to distinguish design from execution. Evil is caused by the free acts of God's creatures, not by God himself. "God is the author of the author of sin, but he cannot be the author of sin itself, for sin is the result of a rebellion against God. Can God rebel against himself?"[5]

Even though God doesn't approve of sin, it's here by his permission. In his omniscience he knew that the plan he chose, even though it included evil, would bring the greatest ultimate good.

While God has not seen fit to reveal all his reasons for allowing evil to come into his perfect creation, at least one of them is clear. Because evil now exists, God can show forth the glory of his grace not only as the Creator of all things but also as the Redeemer. The reality of sin made it necessary for God to send his Son to overcome the power of sin and of death. The crucifixion and resurrection of Jesus Christ were the greatest possible display of God's love, mercy, and holiness to men and angels. God chose the plan that would allow him most completely and effectively to demonstrate the splendor of his attributes.

There are some interesting biblical passages that relate to the problem of evil and how God has permitted it to be a part of his plan. The Lord declares, "I form the light, and create darkness: I make peace, and create evil" (Isa. 45:7 KJV). And, "Shall there be evil in a city, and the LORD hath not done it?" (Amos 3:6 KJV). The words translated *evil* in these verses can also be translated "distress, misery, injury, calamity." God doesn't create injury or calamity for its own sake, but he uses it as an instrument of righteous judgment.

The Bible never blames God for sin. Instead, the Scriptures teach that when sin occurs, God holds the one who commits it responsible. God does not commit evil even though it's under his control. Note two biblical examples.

"Out of your own household I am going to bring calamity upon you. Before your very eyes I will take your wives and give them to one who is close to you, and he will lie with your wives in broad daylight" (2 Sam. 12:11). It would appear at first that God is directly responsible for this evil because he planned it to happen. But when the sin actually takes place (2 Sam. 16:21–22), Ahithophel and Absalom are the ones who are directly responsible. They committed the sin by their own free choice. God didn't force them to do this, yet he was in control of the situation to use it as a punishment for David's sin.

"For God has put it into their hearts to accomplish his purpose by agreeing to give the beast their power to rule, until God's words are fulfilled" (Rev. 17:17). God is clearly in control, but he's not the agent responsible for committing the sin that results. The other part of the picture is in Revelation 13:2, 7–8.

"When moral agents go too far in dallying with evil, God can so move in their own activity that even demonic acts fall in line to promote God's ultimate purposes. God sets limits on evil and even uses it, but he is not complicit in it."6

So God is in sovereign control, but he is also righteous and good. As Paul writes, "But if our unrighteousness brings out God's righteousness more clearly, what shall we say? That God is unjust in bringing his wrath on us? (I am using a human argument.) Certainly not! If that were so, how could God judge the world?" (Rom. 3:5–6; see also Hab. 1:13; James 1:13; 1 John 1:5). God cannot be a fair judge if he himself is to blame for sin in the world.

We said earlier that God is the designer of a plan that included sin, though he's never responsible for committing it. In a way we can compare him to an earthly architect who designs a large building or bridge. Depending on the construction's size and nature, the architect can predict the approximate number of workers who will be killed. The plans obviously don't call for any casualties, but some will be inevitable if the project is large enough. No one will blame the architect for these deaths even though those who died were following his blueprints.

This illustration may help, but it eventually breaks down. Unlike the architect, God is in sovereign control. But his design is so perfect that he can't fairly be blamed for evil. Instead, he will be praised forever for his goodness.

So far we've said much about responsibility, but we've omitted something very important. We need to keep in mind that we're speaking about the Creator of the heavens and earth and all that exists. To whom then is *God* responsible? There are no other gods, and God is answerable to no one but himself.

"Who has understood the mind of the LORD, or instructed him as his counselor? Whom did the LORD consult to enlighten him, and who taught him the right way? Who was it that taught him knowledge or showed him the path of understanding?" (Isa. 40:13–14). The answer is, no one. No creature has a right to judge the Creator. God's response to Job's protest makes this point clear: "Will the one who contends with the Almighty correct him? Let him who accuses God answer him!" (Job 40:2).

This does not mean God is a despot who rules his creatures tyrannically without regard for their best interests. Instead, we need to start with what we know of God's character, especially when we reflect upon the problem of suffering and evil. God's character is the absolute standard for good (see Mark 10:18). It's the changeless criterion for right versus wrong, for righteousness versus sin. This is why sin is best defined as anything contrary to God's character. There's no antecedent principle of goodness or truth to which God must conform. *He* is the absolute for goodness, beauty, and truth. Therefore, God is free to do the whole counsel of his will, and this will lead, by definition, to the greatest good.

Many have objected to this, claiming the God of the Bible isn't good, at least in terms of society's standards. But this doesn't follow since society's moral standards have no foundation apart from the revelatory base of the Bible. As Pinnock says, "Only belief in God can provide the sound basis in reality for that confidence in the final worth of human life which ethics presupposes."[7] The morals of society should be compared to God's standards, not vice versa. Those who refuse to believe that God is good have no basis for morality at all. C. S. Lewis convincingly argues this point:

> Unless we take our own standard of goodness to be valid in principle (however fallible our particular applications of it) we cannot mean anything by calling waste and cruelty evils. And unless we take our own standard to be something more than ours, to be in fact an objective principle to which we're responding, we cannot regard that standard as valid. In a word, *unless we allow ultimate reality to be moral, we cannot morally condemn it* [italics mine].[8]

THE ORIGIN OF EVIL: THE TWO FALLS

God didn't directly create evil, but he did allow it to be a part of his plan. The first order of creatures made by God were spirit beings: the angels. Nature as we know it didn't yet exist since the creation of angels was prior to the creation of the physical universe.

God's creation was good, and all his creatures were perfect. But the angels were created with free will, meaning there was always the genuine possibility of a wrong decision. The angels weren't programmed robots, but moral beings capable of loving and serving God.

Satan and the angels who fell with him reached a point where they chose to prefer themselves to God. This selfishness and pride was the origin of sin and of evil. Many of the angels freely chose to remain faithful to their Creator. The holiness of these angels has been confirmed, and they cannot sin. This doesn't mean that they'll no longer be able to choose; instead, it means that in the fullness of the beatific vision, their obedience to the living God will always be willing and pleasurable.

After Satan's fall he appeared in Eden to tempt man. The second fall, that of man, occurred soon afterward. The two falls are similar because Adam and Eve chose their own way in preference to God's, just as Satan and the other fallen angels had done. The biggest difference between the angelic and human falls is that all the angels were in existence at the time of Satan's sin, while only two humans existed at the time of the second fall. Unlike the angels, humanity was designed to reproduce. And since the parents of the human race became sinners, all their descendants would need redemption. "Therefore, just as sin entered the world through one man, and death through sin, and in this way death came to all men, because all sinned.... For just as through the disobedience of the one man the many were made sinners, so also through the obedience of the one man the many will be made righteous" (Rom. 5:12, 19).

Thus, evil originated not with God but with the two falls. This is the only solution to the problem of evil. Nevertheless, there is an important objection to this biblical solution: *"Couldn't God have made creatures who would always have chosen to do right?"*

Some Christians respond by saying no to this question. They argue that free will makes sin inevitable unless God keeps his creatures humble by specially displaying his glory.

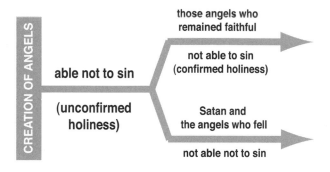

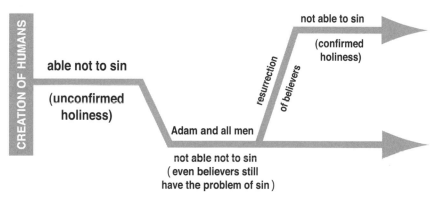

The fall of angels, bringing evil into the cosmos, divided them permanently: the angels—not able to sin; Satan and his angels—not able not to sin. Men, on the other hand, through the fall became evil and are not able not to sin, even as believers. Confirmed holiness—not able to sin—comes only at the resurrection of the believer.

Others say that the question is meaningless because it speaks of a different plan and reality. If God is omniscient and omnipotent, this plan (that includes evil) is the only possible plan since it must be the best. Omniscience requires that God knows what plan would be best, and omnipotence requires that God is able to carry it out. Only if God is not wholly good could he have chosen a plan other than the best.

On the other hand, this question isn't as theoretical as some think. There are two reasons for this: (1) The unfallen angels. Some of God's creatures chose to remain faithful to him, and they continue to do so. In fact they will remain faithful to God throughout all eternity (see Rev. 5:11–14). Does this mean they no longer have free will? (2) Resurrected believers will never sin. God will take away the power of sin so that they can be with God and serve him forever. Will there be no free will in heaven? These two examples make it clear there can be free will without the necessity of sin. Divine sovereignty will coexist with the creatures' freedom for eternity.

If we extend this into the past, we can see that God could have kept his creatures from sinning without interfering with their free will. This is precisely what will happen in heaven. This all boils down to the divine sovereignty/human responsibility mystery. Are we then answering the problem of evil with a mystery? Yes, because if both divine sovereignty and human responsibility are true (as the Bible affirms), then God *is* powerful and completely good even though evil exists. Remember that the truths of a mystery are not contradictory. They only appear to be that way to human comprehension. What we are offering as the solution to the problem of evil is thus a self-consistent explanation based on the original assumption that God has revealed himself to man and that revelation is the Bible.

No matter what God was *able* to do about free will and sin, he is never to blame for the execution of sin if it occurs. As to the question of why God freely chose to include evil in his plan, we must answer that God cannot deny himself; it *must* be the best possible reality. This isn't the best of all possible worlds, but it is the best way to bring about the best of all possible worlds.[9]

Another objection to the biblical free will solution is that it only solves the problem of moral evil. What about natural evil? The answer is that this type of evil is also a product of man's rebellion against God. Many biblical passages about the curse clearly reveal that the present disease-death environment is a direct result of the curse due to the fall of man (see Gen. 3:14–19; Rom. 8:18–23; Rev. 22:3). Nature isn't now as God desires—it is abnormal. The Bible is *unique* in its teaching that death ought never to have occurred. It would appear that there was no death before the Genesis 3 curse (Rom. 5:12; 1 Cor. 15:21).

Even animal pain falls under the curse. Some interpreters hold that before sin entered, there were no carnivorous animals; the animals were all herbivores (Gen. 1:29–30). When the curse is lifted (partially when Christ reigns on earth and completely at the creation of the new heavens and new earth), the animals will once again become herbivores (Isa. 11:6–9). Nature itself will be redeemed when God's children are resurrected (Rom. 8:18–23), and this resurrection is possible because Jesus rose from the dead. Since sin brought the curse of death, when sin is removed, the curse also will be removed.

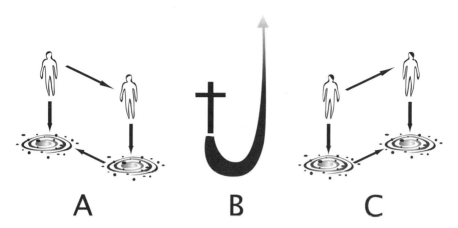

A. Because Adam fell, the universe likewise was cursed, for fallen man could not have dominion over an unfallen creation.
B. Christ's substitutionary death and resurrection will finally remove death and the curse.
C. When we are raised and glorified, the curse will also be removed, and nature will be redeemed (Rom. 8:19–23).

Thus, to paraphrase Francis Schaeffer, God can be furious with natural and moral evil without being angry with himself.[10] God didn't create man as he now is, for otherwise God would be evil for creating a cruel and sinful creature. Instead, the Bible teaches that man changed just as the fallen angels changed. The uniquely biblical teaching of the two falls is the only real explanation to the problem of evil.

GOD'S SOLUTION FOR EVIL: THE WORK OF CHRIST

From beginning to end, the Bible consistently says that while evil is real, God is nevertheless omnipotent and good. In fact, evil is God's enemy, and he is suffering because of the sin and wickedness that exist in the hearts of Adam's sons and daughters.

THE PROBLEM OF EVIL

Some Proposed Solutions	The Biblical Data
1. God's goodness is different from man's goodness.	1. God is sovereign and omnipotent.
2. All evils are punishments for sin.	2. God created beings with genuine free will.
3. God is somehow "beyond" good and evil.	3. God is not the author of sin and evil, nor is he responsible for them.
4. The problem of evil is exaggerated.	4. The beings who sinned deserved full blame for the evil that resulted.
5. Evil is only an illusion.	5. God allows evil to continue until the end of all things.
6. God is struggling against evil, but he is not omnipotent.	6. Jesus Christ and his work on the cross are God's solution to the problem of evil.

God is aware of men's troubles and needs, and in his love he has done something about them. He sent his own Son to die and pay for sin. Jesus Christ came to face and overcome evil as the sinless God-man (1 John 3:8). Though man brought death through his rebellion, God came to earth to give life, not willing to let sin, disease, and death have the last word. In this way he proved he loved us (Rom. 5:8; 1 John 4:9–10).

God chose a plan that included the suffering and death of his Son. It is obvious God wasn't simply amusing himself when he created the heavens and earth. But Carnell adds, "The crucifixion, *the worst example of evil,* was not only permitted by God; *it was sovereignly decreed.*"[11] This "worst example of evil" was included in God's plan from before the foundation of the earth, but as in the case of all other evils, God wasn't responsible for carrying it out. "It could hardly be argued that those who crucified Christ didn't sin because God used the crucifixion to save mankind."[12]

Hell in Light of the Greatest Good

The Bible makes it clear that in the future there will be no grayness or neutrality. We use shades of gray, but the Scriptures use the contrast of black and white. Heaven and hell are the only options. But the doctrine of hell seems so fantastic that many object to it, saying a loving and good God cannot send people to an eternal punishment.

Those who wish to avoid the doctrine of eternal punishment usually suggest either that all men will be saved (universalism) or that the rebellious will be annihilated. These aren't true options, however, as the testimony of Jesus and the rest of the New Testament proves. Some of the phrases the New Testament uses to describe hell are "eternal punishment" (Matt. 25:46), where "their worm does not die, and the fire is not quenched" (Mark 9:48), "weeping and gnashing of teeth" (Matt. 25:30), "eternal fire" (Matt. 25:41), and "for whom blackest darkness has been reserved forever" (Jude v. 13; see also Matt. 7:13; 2 Thess. 1:9; Rev. 14:11).

Hell is eternal, and this means that evil will continue in some form. As C. S. Lewis says:

> I willingly believe that the damned are, in one sense, successful, rebels to the end; that the doors of hell are locked on the *inside*. I don't mean that the ghosts may not *wish* to come out of hell, in the vague fashion wherein an envious man "wishes" to be happy: but they certainly do not will even the first preliminary stages of that self-abandonment through which alone the soul can reach any good. They enjoy forever the horrible freedom they've demanded, and are therefore self-enslaved just as the blessed, forever submitting to obedience, become through all eternity more and more free.[13]

Because of God's omniscience, omnipotence, and goodness, we can be sure that from all eternity he has worked out that plan that will bring the greatest good. True, it's a plan that cost him dearly, not only because the sin of his creatures causes him to suffer, but also because Christ paid an infinite purchase price to redeem sinful men.

Moses says, "The secret things belong to the LORD our God" (Deut. 29:29). We don't know all God's purposes for including evil in his plan, but the Bible does indicate some of them. The main purpose for creation is so God might display the riches of his glory to creatures who can willingly respond. Since God is worthy of all blessing, honor, glory, and dominion (Rev. 5:13), the plan that would bring the greatest good for all is the plan that most freely allows God to display and receive glory. And God knew that the best way to reveal the glory of his grace, love, and holiness would be to redeem wicked, hateful, and rebellious creatures from their course of destruction.

Because of Christ's blood, God can transform sinful rebels into the image of his Son perfectly. The crucifixion was the most complete revelation of God's attributes. If evil didn't appear, the crucifixion and resurrection would have been unnecessary, and there would have been no such thing as redemption. Was it worth all this? Even before God created time, space, and matter, divine omniscience knew what would come to pass.

No one can see the whole picture as God sees it. From our perspective it would appear that many things are out of God's control. But we must place our trust in him. God has revealed that he is guiding everything toward a glorious and purposeful consummation. When we finally see what he's been doing, *we will be satisfied*. We'll learn how divine sovereignty and human responsibility can both be true and there will be no problem of evil.

God's justice will be vindicated, and all creatures will bow to God's holiness (Phil. 2:9–11). No one in hell will call God unfair, and there will be no tears or sorrow in heaven (Rev. 21:4).

God has counted and underwritten the cost of this creation. He is both Creator and Redeemer, and for this he will forever receive all praise (Rev. 4:11; 5:9–10, 12–13).

SOME IMPLICATIONS

Most people who complain about evil are doing little about it themselves. Before any of us try to blame God, we ought to examine ourselves. We need to acknowledge that personal sin is the problem of evil we really should be dealing with. Non-Christians need to turn to Christ for forgiveness of sins, and Christians need to walk by the Spirit and stop serving the flesh (Gal. 5:16). Believers must "grow in the grace and knowledge of our Lord and Savior Jesus Christ" (2 Peter 3:18). It is interesting that the more Christlike a believer grows by God's grace, the more he becomes aware of God's holiness and the sinfulness of sin. The better one knows God, the smaller the problem of evil becomes.

Another personal implication concerns disease, suffering, and death. Many times we'll be tempted to rebel against God because of something that has happened. When things happen to us that seem cruel or unfair, we should remember in all things God has a sovereign purpose.

The most important thing is not the situation but our response to it. Keep in mind suffering has a purpose (1 Peter 2:20–21; 4:1), it's not permanent (Rom. 8:18), and it should be expected (1 Peter 4:12–14). We need to keep a divine perspective in order to respond to life's events properly.

Christ was the ultimate example of innocent suffering, but look at his response: "To this you were called, because Christ suffered for you, leaving you an example, that you should follow in his steps. 'He committed no sin, and no deceit was found in his mouth.' When they hurled their insults at him, he did not retaliate; when he suffered, he made no threats. Instead he entrusted himself to him who judges justly" (1 Peter 2:21–23).

It is good to praise the LORD
and make music to your name, O Most High,
to proclaim your love in the morning
and your faithfulness at night. (Ps. 92:1–2)

I will exalt you, my God the King;
I will praise your name for ever and ever.
Every day I will praise you
and extol your name for ever and ever.

Great is the LORD and most worthy of praise;
his greatness no one can fathom.
One generation will commend your works to another;
they will tell of your mighty acts.
They will speak of the glorious splendor of your majesty,
and I will meditate on your wonderful works.
They will tell of the power of your awesome works,
and I will proclaim your great deeds.
They will celebrate your abundant goodness
and joyfully sing of your righteousness.

The LORD is gracious and compassionate,
slow to anger and rich in love.
The LORD is good to all;
he has compassion on all he has made. (Ps. 145:1–9)

The LORD is righteous in all his ways
and loving toward all he has made.
The LORD is near to all who call on him,
to all who call on him in truth.
He fulfills the desires of those who fear him;
he hears their cry and saves them.
The LORD watches over all who love him,
but all the wicked he will destroy.

My mouth will speak in praise of the LORD.
Let every creature praise his holy name
for ever and ever. (Ps. 145:17–21)

THIRTY YEARS LATER

- Accepting the fact of evil is an essential aspect of becoming a Christian. The conviction by the Holy Spirit of sin, righteousness, and judgment (John 16:8) is necessary to salvation, since people who believe they're basically good will not embrace the gospel of grace. The humanistic assumption of man's basic goodness also spills over into the non-Christian religions and cults, since these are all works based. To admit the depravity of the human heart is to despair of any endeavor of self-salvation. "I do not nullify the grace of God, for if righteousness comes through the Law, then Christ died needlessly" (Gal. 2:21 NASB). If salvation through good deeds is possible, Christ's death was a tragic waste. But if not, he is our only hope. Our Lord underscored the fundamental depravity of the human heart when he said, "That which proceeds out of the man, that is what defiles the man. For from within, out of the heart of men, proceed the evil thoughts, fornications, thefts, murders, adulteries, deeds of coveting and wickedness, as well as deceit, sensuality, envy, slander, pride and foolishness. All these evil things proceed from within and defile the man" (Mark 7:20–23 NASB). If this is true, our only hope is a heart transplant—a new heart. Bootstrap theology won't do, since the solution is inside out, not outside in. Our hope is in Christ's imputed righteousness, not external achievement.

- This understanding of human nature is radically opposed to our culture, which makes evil relative by reducing morality to personal preferences and subjective feelings. Our culture necessarily approaches the problems we face on an external level by claiming that our social ills are due to deprivation, not depravity. Thus, we live in a culture of blame. This is precisely the opposite of the biblical vision of the human condition.

- We're both victims and agents; we've been victimized by others' sins, but we're also agents who sin against others. It would be a mistake to reduce us to one or the other.

- The often-used objection to Christianity based on the existence of evil in the world is self-defeating. Without God, there can be no evil; instead, we would be left merely with instinct and conditioning. The existence of real moral evil requires an unchanging absolute for good.

Chapter 6

THE RESURRECTION BODY

The Bible gives us a glimpse into eternity to come. One significant thing about this future eternity is that we'll all receive resurrection bodies. Christ conquered death, and because he was resurrected, *all* people ("both the righteous and the wicked," Acts 24:15; John 5:29) will be resurrected.

Though the Scriptures don't tell us much about this resurrection body, it is evident that its nature is beyond our present comprehension. The biblical descriptions of this body often sound fantastic, and the more we read about it, the more it appears that we're dealing with another biblical mystery.

God has revealed something about the state of his people's future existence to strengthen the believer's hope and to show he plans to redeem the entire man. But the revelation is limited, because he doesn't want us continually looking at the clouds and ignoring the present work (see Acts 1:11). What he has told us is important because we'll have these bodies for all eternity. Our hope for the future should encourage us in the present.

THE RESURRECTION BODY

The nature of the resurrection body is a somewhat controversial subject. Many deny that the fleshly body will be resurrected. Some claim that this new body will be entirely spiritual. They use 1 Corinthians 15:44 ("it is raised a spiritual body") and 15:50 ("flesh and blood cannot inherit the kingdom of God") to support this view. Confusing the issue is a misunderstanding of *flesh* as it's used in the Bible. Since "the flesh" is intrinsically opposed to the Holy Spirit and vice versa (see Rom. 8:5–8; Gal. 5:17), those who hold this view say, "How can the flesh partake in the resurrection?"

What does the Bible teach about the flesh? According to the Old Testament, the body of flesh is God-given and ethically neutral. Moses says that before the fall there was nothing wrong with man's flesh (see Gen. 1—2). God considered man his "very good" creation, flesh and all. After the fall, the source of sin was said to be in man's heart (the inner, true person), not in his flesh (the outward, visible person). It was sin in the heart that became visible in the flesh.

The term *flesh* in the New Testament is used various ways. Sometimes it refers to the flesh of our bodies (Luke 24:39); sometimes for the whole person, a living being (Acts 2:17 [literal]); sometimes as a synonym for body (Matt. 26:41); sometimes for the power or law of sin (Rom. 7:23; 8:4; see also 3:20); and sometimes for humanity (1 John 4:2). Only when *flesh* is used to mean the power of sin is it intrinsically evil. So Scriptures that condemn "the flesh" really have no relevance to the question of bodily resurrection.

The Old Testament is progressive in its revelation of the resurrection body. Job 19:25–27 is one of the earliest passages used to support the resurrection. Though this passage may imply a resurrection in a body of flesh, there are interpretive problems in this text that make it difficult to be sure. The same is true of Psalms 16:9–11 and 17:15.[1]

Isaiah, however, gives a more direct picture of a bodily resurrection as symbolic of Israel's restoration: "Your dead will live; their bodies will rise. You who dwell in the dust, wake up and shout for joy. Your dew is like the dew of the morning; the earth will give birth to her dead" (26:19).

The clearest Old Testament passage is Daniel 12:2–3: "Multitudes who sleep in the dust of the earth will awake: some to everlasting life, others to shame and everlasting contempt. Those who are wise will shine like the brightness of the heavens, and those who lead many to righteousness, like the stars for ever and ever." Verse 3 is especially interesting because it suggests a dramatic change in the bodies of the saints. They'll consist of glorified flesh.

This resurrection is bodily, not just spiritual, and this whole concept is in direct opposition to Greek thought. The Greeks held that matter is intrinsically evil, a restriction from which the soul must escape. They looked for the immortality of the soul rather than the whole man. The Bible, however, attributes a real dignity to the human body. It is the temple of the Holy Spirit, if one is a Christian, and thus we can glorify God in our bodies.

THE RESURRECTION BODY OF JESUS CHRIST

The Scriptures say Jesus Christ's resurrection body is the pattern for the believer's resurrection body. "If we have been united with him like this in his death, we will certainly also be united with him in his resurrection" (Rom. 6:5).

In writing to the Philippians, Paul makes this point even clearer: "But our citizenship is in heaven. And we eagerly await a Savior from there, the Lord Jesus Christ, who, by the power that enables him to bring everything under his control, will *transform our lowly bodies so that they will be like his glorious body*" (3:20–21).

The apostle John expresses the same truth: "Dear friends, now we are children of God, and what we will be has not yet been made known. But we know that when he appears, we shall be like him, for we shall see him as he is" (1 John 3:2). Therefore, to discover the characteristics of our future bodies, we need to look at the characteristics of Christ's risen body.

Christ's resurrection body reflects and bears God's glory. At this time, the Lord "alone is immortal and ... lives in unapproachable light" (1 Tim. 6:16). While some people have been raised from the dead before and since Christ, none of them received resurrection bodies. Lazarus and others were only resuscitated; their bodies were restored to life, but they died again.

Christ is the only one who has permanently conquered the grave by receiving a glorified resurrection body. This is why he is appropriately called "the firstfruits" (1 Cor. 15:20, 23) and "the firstborn from among the dead" (Col. 1:18; Rev. 1:5). Because Christ is the firstfruits, we know that the harvest will be in kind.[2]

As we consider the characteristics of Christ's resurrected body, we will see that we're running into facts we can't fully comprehend. Somehow, Christ's body is completely substantial yet glorified. It's identified with his preresurrection body—yet different.

A Substantial Body

We know from the Gospels and Acts that Christ's resurrected body is real and substantial. His body could be handled. Matthew records how his disciples "clasped his feet and worshiped him" (28:9). Christ himself said, "Look at my hands and my feet. It is I myself! Touch me and see; a ghost does not have flesh and bones, as you see I have" (Luke 24:39). (The phrase *flesh and bones* has led to some speculation that Jesus' resurrection body doesn't have blood. But to say he has flesh and bones does not exclude the possibility that his body has blood also. Flesh and bones are the most solid parts of the body, and Jesus referred to them to prove to the doubting disciples that his body was real.)

The whole narrative in Luke 24:13–32 depicts Jesus as a real person with a physical body. He walked and talked with two disciples on the way to Emmaus, broke bread, and gave it to them. Christ took and ate a piece of broiled fish in the disciples' sight (Luke 24:41–43; see also Acts 10:40–41). His body did not *need* the fish (see 1 Cor. 6:13), but he could eat it nonetheless.

Further evidence that Christ's risen body is physical can be seen in John 20:17. He told Mary to stop clinging to him because he hadn't yet ascended to the Father. This doesn't mean his resurrection body was so glorious that it was untouchable. Instead, he may have meant that "she must cease clinging to him, trying to keep him always with her. Jesus is about to ascend to the Father and from then on the fellowship with him will be of a different sort."[3]

John tells us Christ breathed on the disciples and later invited Thomas to touch his hands and side (John 20:22, 27). It's also clear that Christ's body sometimes looked like his earthly body, because his disciples recognized him (see Matt. 28:9, 17).

A Glorified Body

This is the other side of this mystery. There are many strange qualities that are hard to reconcile with the fact that Christ's body is substantial. For instance, most of those who saw Christ after his resurrection were unable to recognize him at first. Christ had to say or do something before those to whom he appeared could be certain that it was he. Mary mistook him for a gardener until he called her by name. The two disciples on the way to Emmaus were with him for a considerable time before they recognized him at his breaking of the bread. Evidently the risen Lord could change his form and appearance at will (Mark 16:12).

It is also clear that Jesus could vanish (Luke 24:31). Also, he wasn't limited to space or time because he could move immediately from place to place by an act of will, as marvelously demonstrated by his ascension (Acts 1:9). Jesus in his risen body could handle objects (Luke 24:30) yet could be independent of them. We can see this in the way he was able to pass through closed doors when he appeared to the disciples (John 20:19).

We know Christ's body is perfect and that it is a spiritual body, meaning it is permeated and empowered by the Holy Spirit. Because of this, Christ's resurrection body is imbued with glorious qualities that he demonstrated before his ascension. It's adapted to the magnificent environment that is yet to come. Therefore, what's normal for this body of the new creation would appear miraculous to any observer today.

The New Testament suggests Christ may usually have been invisible even while on earth prior to the ascension. He only appeared during those forty days on certain occasions (see Paul's partial list of appearances in 1 Cor. 15:5–8). This may imply that when Christ is not accommodating his body to mortal sight he can't be seen unless the observer is himself in a resurrection body.

One last question remains: Did Jesus' ascension bring about such a change that he ceased to have a glorified body of flesh? This is very important because it's difficult to combine what we know of Christ's risen body before the ascension with the picture we find after his ascension. Christ now dwells with the Father "in unapproachable light" (1 Tim. 6:16). This is evident from the awesome though symbolic description recorded in Revelation 1:12–18 and his blinding appearance to Paul on the Damascus road (Acts 9:1–9).

However, none of this means that the Lord Jesus is no longer in a glorified body of flesh. On the contrary, Christ retained the same form after his ascension: "Jesus, who has been taken from you into heaven, will come back in the same way you have seen him go into heaven" (Acts 1:11).

Apparently then, Christ willfully held back his true glory and light while he was in the presence of sinful men on the earth after the resurrection. No mortal eyes would have been able to stand the intensity of his glory if he had not done this. He is still in his resurrection body of glorified flesh as he will forever be.

THE RESURRECTION BODY OF THE BELIEVER

In the not-distant future, "we shall be like him" (1 John 3:2) and conformed "with the body of His glory" (Phil. 3:21 NASB). Every believer will receive a glorified body because of Jesus' redemptive work.

One of the unique teachings of the Bible is that death was never meant to be a part of the natural course of events. It's an unnatural phenomenon brought about by sin. When we're resurrected, we'll be delivered from our bondage to sin, and being made sinless we will abide with the Lord forever.

First Corinthians 15

In the central passage on the believer's bodily resurrection, the apostle Paul presents Christ's resurrection as the basis of the believer's hope of resurrection. He speaks of two representative men, the first and last Adams. The first Adam (vv. 21–22, 45) brought death, but the last Adam is the Redeemer who conquers death and brings life.

Then Paul says,

> But someone may ask, "How are the dead raised? With what kind of body will they come?" How foolish! What you sow does not come to life unless it dies. When you sow, you do not plant the body that will be, but just a seed, perhaps of wheat or of something else. But God gives it a body as he has determined, and to each kind of seed he gives its own body. (vv. 35–38)

The Corinthians evidently had a problem with the concept of a bodily resurrection. The Hellenistic influence was strong and led many to doubt the whole idea. The questions Paul asks are the objections some of the Corinthians were raising (v. 35). Paul answers by saying there will be a substantial continuity between the present body and the resurrection body, just as there is a continuity between a seed and the plant that grows from it. This is a powerful illustration if you stop to consider the miraculous transformation of a tiny seed into a full-grown plant. In the same way, we'll be transformed and glorified, yet we'll still be recognizable.

Each person will have his own unique resurrection body. The present body is the seed from which the new body will be patterned, but the new body will vastly excel the present body in an incomprehensible way. We can't clearly discern from Scripture how similar our resurrected bodies will be to our present bodies (but see Isa. 35:5–6).

The next section of 1 Corinthians 15 (vv. 39–41) builds on the previous illustration of how God is able to bring dead bodies to a new and incomparably greater life. Here Paul illustrates from the variety of God's creation his ability to create bodies with different degrees of glory. God can make various bodies suitable to different conditions, and the present creation shows that he is able to transform our earthly bodies into glorified heavenly bodies. Daniel tells us, in fact, that these new bodies will rival the stars themselves in brightness (12:3).

Paul continues the metaphor of the sowing and raising of seed in verses 42–49 with a series of sharp contrasts between the present body and the resurrected body:

1. perishable—imperishable
2. dishonor—glory
3. weakness—power
4. natural—spiritual
5. the first man Adam (a living soul)—the last Adam (a life-giving spirit)
6. earthly—heavenly
7. mortal—immortal (vv. 53–54)

Unlike our present bodies, our new bodies will not be frail. They will be characterized by great power and glory while remaining corporeal and substantial. Jesus makes it clear that the new body will be a body of flesh, since this was true of his own body (Luke 24:39), but it won't be bound to the earth by its flesh, as it is now. Our present mortal and corruptible body isn't suitable to the future heavenly existence. Our bodies must be transformed into imperishable bodies of glorified flesh in order to fit in the new environment.

The rest of the passage (and also 1 Thess. 4:14–18) describes how the resurrection will be happen instantaneously. It's not a process and it's not going on today. The "mystery" Paul speaks of (v. 51) is the new revelation that some people will never die at all. Those Christians who are alive when Christ comes for his church will be instantly changed into their immortal bodies. The victory over death, according to Paul, isn't deliverance from the body, but redemption of the body.

The Goal of the Redemptive Process

The necessity for the resurrection body is to perfect man in the flesh and reveal our sonship. When we are glorified, all restrictions will be removed, so we can truly reflect the divine image and thus glorify God.

Two extremes relating to this mystery must be avoided. One is to say that the new body is the same as the old. This would be mere resuscitation, "warts and all."[4] The Pharisees moved in this direction and brought the doctrine of the bodily resurrection down to a basely material level. They disputed whether a person would rise in exactly the same clothes in which he was buried.[5] The Athenians probably misunderstood Paul to be promoting this type of teaching when he began to speak about the resurrection of the dead in Acts 17:31–32.

The second extreme is to say that the new body is entirely different from the old. Many infer that resurrection is a continuation of life after death in the form of an ethereal spirit existence. As mentioned earlier, the Greeks thought the flesh to be evil and not worthy of resurrection. They hated the idea of the redemption of the body because they didn't have the special revelation that the new body would be divested of the limitations caused by sin.

The Bible reveals that we will be set free from the conflict of sin when we're in our new bodies. Many religions only offer loss of individual personality (absorption into the ocean of being or the universe's "life force") as their "hope." Those who teach reincarnation think of the body as a prison from which the soul needs to be liberated. But the Bible offers forgiveness and future liberation from sin through a redeemed and glorified body, made possible by Christ's death and resurrection.

Some people deny the bodily resurrection because they fear a conflict with science. They erect ludicrous pictures of God searching the universe to collect the individual atoms that once made up the bodies of the departed dead (in spite of the fact that the chemical constitution of our bodies is constantly changing). But the God who created matter and energy, space and time, reveals that he will create resurrection bodies "in a flash, in the twinkling of an eye" (1 Cor. 15:52). These new bodies will belong to a new order of physics.

Summary of Features

1. The resurrection body is a spiritual body, designed to exist in the new heavens and new earth;
2. it consists of glorified flesh;
3. it is a perfect body—it can't become diseased or die;
4. it can't be fatigued since it's imbued with the power of the Holy Spirit and thus will probably not require sleep;
5. it won't require food for subsistence (see 1 Cor. 6:13), but it can eat and assimilate food;
6. like the angels (Matt. 22:30; Luke 20:35), we "will neither marry nor be given in marriage" (since we won't die, there's no need to reproduce);
7. the resurrection body will be recognizable (1 Thess. 2:19; 4:17), though to an extent it may be able to change its form and appearance at will;
8. it may be able to move instantly from place to place;
9. it will be brilliant, reflecting God's glory (Dan. 12:3);
10. it won't be subject to the same experiential restrictions of time and space as now;
11. it will be free from all sin;
12. the ability to appreciate, worship, and understand the things of God will be much increased, because the mind will be freed from the errors and restraints caused by sin;
13. we'll be above the angels in God's order (see 1 Cor. 6:3);
14. the body will have supernatural abilities; what's normal to that body would appear miraculous to us now, since it's a body of the new creation;
15. each new body will be unique, yet the body of Christ will still be a corporate entity, the whole body being resurrected at once;
16. it can be seen and touched, but it may be able to vanish or appear at will.

THE RESURRECTION BODY

THE RESURRECTION BODY OF JESUS CHRIST

- A substantial body
- A glorified body
- A recognizable body
- A completely different body
- A perfect body

THE RESURRECTION BODY OF THE BELIEVER

1. Is a spiritual body
2. Consists of glorified flesh
3. Is a perfect body
4. Will not require sleep
5. Will not require food
6. Will not marry or reproduce
7. Will be recognizable
8. Can move instantly from place to place
9. Will be brilliant, relecting God's glory
10. Will not be subject to time and space restrictions
11. Will be free from all sin
12. Will have an increased capacity to appreciate, worship, and understand God and his revelation
13. Will be above the angels
14. Will have supernatural abilities
15. Each will be unique yet part of the body of Christ
16. Can be seen and touched but will be able to vanish and appear at will

SOME IMPLICATIONS

1. *We will understand many things that are now incomprehensible.* The resurrection body, for instance, will be fully explained only when it is experienced. Until that time, "what we will be has not yet been made known" (1 John 3:2). We don't presently have the categories to relate to the nature of the resurrection body. How could you describe a color to one born blind?

When we're resurrected, many of the things we now must call mysteries will become comprehensible. "In that day you will no longer ask me anything"

(John 16:23). Our minds are now darkened by the presence of sin, but when it's removed, our minds will be free to function more clearly. Our hearts will rejoice in that day.

> 2. *Our true desires will be fulfilled.* The biblical teaching of the redemption and resurrection of the *whole* person offers the answer to our deepest longings. God is the one who alone can perfectly complete us through the redemptive work of his Son.

Spiritually, our propensity to sin will be taken away, and we'll be restored to perfect fellowship with the living God. Augustine declared that "Thou hast formed us for Thyself, and our hearts are restless till they find rest in Thee." When we see God, our restlessness will turn into satisfaction and joy.

Mentally, our ability to comprehend and grasp God's truth will be increased.

Emotionally, our passions will be pure and sinless. Our fellowship and love for God will be reflected in intimate love and complete unity among all believers.

Physically, the troubles and distractions caused by the constant demands of weak and dying bodies will disappear. We won't get tired or diseased, and there may be no need of sleep. It may be unnecessary to spend time traveling from one place to another. We won't have to worry about clothing. As for food, we'll no longer have to labor in cultivating, buying, and preparing meals. We won't even have to wash dishes or dispose of garbage and sewage!

Even the little nuisances of life will evidently be gone (for instance, the Murphy's Law idea that "if something can go wrong, it will"). The changes will be so far reaching we won't be ready for such a new level of life until we're resurrected.

> 3. *We can have real comfort now.* Throughout the Scriptures, the doctrine of the resurrection is used to provide a genuine hope for the future. Now we know God by faith, but then we'll know him face-to-face. Many of us may suffer now, but then we'll realize that "the sufferings of this present time are not worthy to be compared with the glory that is to be revealed to us" (Rom. 8:18 NASB; see 2 Cor. 4:17).

Even though we are now surrounded by the reality of death, we can have peace and comfort in the knowledge that death will soon be swallowed up in victory. By faith believers can say with Paul, "Where, O death, is your victory? Where, O death, is your sting?" (1 Cor. 15:55).

4.   *We will conquer the present restrictions of time and space.* Our experience of time and space will be different when we're in our resurrected bodies. They will no longer be as restrictive as they are now. We'll evidently be ageless, and we may have immediate access to all parts of the universe. Our hopes of exploring the distant mysteries of space will be realized.

Time and space—these are the fascinating subjects of our next chapters.

> I am still confident of this:
> I will see the goodness of the LORD
> in the land of the living.
> Wait for the LORD;
> be strong and take heart
> and wait for the LORD. (Ps. 27:13–14)

> Surely goodness and love will follow me
> all the days of my life,
> and I will dwell in the house of the LORD
> forever. (Ps. 23:6)

> Therefore we do not lose heart. Though outwardly we are wasting away, yet inwardly we are being renewed day by day. For our light and momentary troubles are achieving for us an eternal glory that far outweighs them all. So we fix our eyes not on what is seen, but on what is unseen. For what is seen is temporary, but what is unseen is eternal. (2 Cor. 4:16–18)

> And the God of all grace, who called you to his eternal glory in Christ, after you have suffered a little while, will himself restore you

and make you strong, firm and steadfast. To him be the power for ever and ever. Amen. (1 Peter 5:10–11)

THIRTY YEARS LATER

- I've come to think of heaven as endless, creative activity without frustration to God's glory. We won't be bored in heaven. Instead, our earthly experiences of creativity, intimacy, adventure, and beauty point beyond themselves to their ultimate fulfillment in our Father's house. These are only hints of home, or what C. S. Lewis called "'patches of Godlight' in the woods of our experience" in *Letters to Malcolm: Chiefly on Prayer*. Conversely, our earthly experiences of disappointment, alienation, boredom, and ugliness are reminders that we are not home yet.
- Texts like Romans 8:18–39; 2 Corinthians 4:16–18; James 1:2–12; and 1 Peter 1:3–9; 4:12–19 remind us it's wise to see we're pilgrims, sojourners, strangers, and aliens in exile in this fleeting world. As people who have trusted in Christ, the longest time period we'll have to suffer pain, loss, and grief is a few decades. This isn't to trivialize our pain in this life, but to put it in context (Heb. 12:2–3; 1 Cor. 15:51–58).
- An excerpt from my *Conformed to His Image* is apropos:

    The Scriptures paint a sobering and realistic portrait of the human condition. People delude themselves with short-term aspirations and pleasures, but a brutally honest analysis of life on this side of the grave without hope on the other side would lead to despair. If death ends all, human life is a mere incident in an indifferent universe, a meaningless blip in cosmic time.

    Near the end of his life, Aldous Huxley, author of *Brave New World*, arrived at this conclusion: "It is a bit embarrassing to have been concerned with the human problem all one's life and find at the end that one has no more to offer by way of advice than 'Try to be a little kinder.'" Without God, humanistic answers to the questions of earthly existence ultimately reduce to naive bromides and platitudes.

In "My Speech to the Graduates," Woody Allen confronted this dilemma with ironic humor: "More than any other time in history, mankind faces a crossroads. One path leads to despair and utter hopelessness. The other, to total extinction. Let us pray we have the wisdom to choose correctly. I speak, by the way, not with any sense of futility but with a panicky conviction of the absolute meaning-lessness of human existence which could easily be misinterpreted as pessimism."[6] This ironic statement by Woody Allen is simultaneously humorous and tragic, depicting as it does the corporate and individual human condition without a transcendent and timeless foundation for meaning.

Ecclesiastes 3:11 tells us that God has set eternity in our hearts. Since this is so, people have deeply embedded desires for meaning and fulfillment that no natural happiness will satisfy. In *The Weight of Glory*, C. S. Lewis observed that "almost our whole education has been directed to silencing this shy, persistent, inner voice; almost all our modern philosophies have been devised to convince us that the good of man is to be found on this earth." Someone noted that while people in our culture are reading the *Times*, we should be reading the eternities. The more we develop a biblical perspective, the clearer we see the true emptiness and hopelessness of people without Christ.

- Elsewhere in *Conformed to His Image*, I observed the implications of the three dominant worldviews vying for our allegiance. The first claims that ultimate reality is material and that everything in the universe is the unintended by-product of time and chance within an impersonal cosmos. There are variations of this view, but it is best known as naturalism, atheism, and humanism.

The second worldview claims that ultimate reality isn't material, but spiritual. However, this spiritual agent isn't a personal being, but the all-that-is. Variations of this view include monism, pantheism, transcendentalism, and the whole New Age movement.

Theism, the third worldview, distinguishes between the creation and the Creator and declares that ultimate reality is an infinite, intelligent, and personal Being. Christian theism affirms that this personal God has decisively revealed himself in the person and work of Jesus Christ.

Only the third worldview offers genuine hope beyond the grave, since the first predicts annihilation, and the second, reincarnation. Contrary to the pop version of reincarnation in the West, Eastern religions teach reincarnation is undesirable, since it brings us around and around on the painful wheel of life. Instead, the Eastern vision of salvation is absorption into the ocean of being. But this isn't a vision of personal consciousness or relationship; it's simply a spiritual version of annihilation.

Instead of annihilation or reincarnation, the Scriptures teach resurrection into an eternally new existence of light, life, and love characterized by intimacy with our Lord and one another. Everything we go through now will be more than worth it in the end, because the divine Architect of the universe, the God and Father of our Lord Jesus Christ, never builds a staircase that leads nowhere.

- Believers who die before the Lord's return will be disembodied. This is an intermediate heavenly existence in the presence of the Lord until their souls/spirits are united with a glorious and permanent resurrection body (1 Thess. 4:13–18).
- Although the Scriptures don't tell us, it is possible we'll somehow be ageless in our resurrected appearance, neither young nor old. If so, those who died before reaching maturity in this world will be like those who did mature, and those who grew old and infirm will no longer be withered but ageless.

Chapter 7

TIME

T ime is a great mystery. All of us interact with it and talk about it, but time is something that defies real definition. It flows along like a silent river carrying the movement of events and experiences.

What do clocks and watches really measure? In some ways time is the measure of motion, but in other ways motion seems to measure time. Since everything in our universe is in motion, we must pick something (usually the sun) as a point of reference and measure our time in relation to it.

But time deals with more than events, experiences, and motion. It also relates to different states of being. Each of us has a past, present, and future through which we're constantly changing. And we all share time in common, even though we often do not experience the passing of time in the same way. One's experience of how time passes depends on each situation.

Most of us naturally think of time in one dimension, moving in a linear way from past to present to future. This abstraction fits well with most experiences, but many evidences argue that there is more to time than this. Time is a relative thing, and there may be different kinds of time. The whole subject is difficult to approach because human perception of time is faulty and limited.

What does the Bible say about time? This chapter will discuss the biblical teaching on time and how it relates to human history and God. We'll discover that God's relationship to time is another mystery, since it's incomprehensible to the human mind.

TIME AND PHYSICS

Scientific techniques and fields of exploration have become so sophisticated that it's become necessary to break time and space into smaller and smaller units. Hours were long since broken into minutes and minutes into seconds. But recently even the second became much too large for many purposes. Scientists have now developed laser clocks, which can measure pulses of light as short as three-tenths of a trillionth of a second!

But in spite of this technical progress, science has been discovering that the universe is more puzzling and mysterious than we ever could have imagined. For instance, physicists and astronomers are now speculating about quasars and black holes in space-time. They're also working with the problems of anti-matter, antiparticles, negative mass, and imaginary mass.

And then there's that strangest of all particles, the neutrino. The neutrino may have essentially *no physical properties*. It has no electric charge, no magnetic field, and isn't affected by gravitational or electromagnetic fields. Billions of neutrinos constantly stream like a thick rain *right through the earth* as though it were not there.[1]

Even light itself can't really be comprehended because of its dual nature, consisting of waves and yet particles. Many of the phenomena just mentioned defy definition in terms of substance, space, and time. The more we examine the universe, the more we begin to see what a strange and complex wonderland it is. Consider the greatness of the God who created all this out of nothing, and then try to imagine what creation will be like when it's released from slavery to the Adamic curse.

Traditional concepts of time have also suffered severe wounds at the hands of modern physics. Newton thought time was something absolute, flowing "equably without relation to anything external." This meant that what we call *now* is not only our now but also the now for the entire universe.[2] Things that occupy the same point in Newton's absolute time are completely simultaneous.

Albert Einstein, however, discarded this idea of absolute time in his special and general theories of relativity. Einstein held that man's sense of time, like his sense of color, is a form of perception. It's therefore subjective and intuitive. We try to objectify time by measuring it with clocks and calendars, but we should remember that all clocks relate to the motion of our solar system. "What we call an hour is actually a measurement in space—an arc of 15 degrees in the apparent daily rotation of the celestial sphere."[3] Time is always dependent on the system of reference.

Time, then, is subjective and relative, but this doesn't mean that time doesn't exist. Time is real, and it's definitely affected by gravitational fields and velocity. One of the most fascinating implications of special relativity is that physical processes go slower in objects when they travel at high speeds. Time would actually expand for the person who could somehow travel close to the speed of light.

This idea has led to some interesting hypothetical space trips. James Reid, for instance, describes a trip to the star Alpha Centauri.[4] With today's rocket speeds, a round-trip to this star (about 8.7 light-years) would require centuries. If the relativity of time didn't hold true, this trip would be too long even if the spacecraft could travel at or near the speed of light.

But because of relativity, the trip would only take *one month* for the travelers if their ship had a velocity of 99.995 percent of the speed of light (186,000 miles per second). But during this one-month period, people on earth would have aged about ten years! Under these conditions time would flow at *two different rates* at the same "time." Thus, the people on the spaceship would be time travelers as well as space travelers. In one month they would have journeyed ten years into the future with respect to earth.

A two-month round-trip to the center of our Milky Way Galaxy (made possible by velocities a little closer to the speed of light) would be a journey of 54,000 light-years to earthlings. The space-time travelers would return to an earth about 60,000 years older than when they left! If people on earth could somehow view the travelers on TV, they would have to watch for about a month and a half to get the equivalent of ten seconds on the spaceship. It would take days to detect any movement at all. But from the astronaut's perspective, people on earth would be moving so fast that they would be invisible blurs.

This illustration is particularly interesting when connected with 2 Peter 3:8: "But do not forget this one thing, dear friends: With the Lord a day is like a thousand years, and a thousand years are like a day." In this relativity example, one day with the space traveler is the equivalent of 1,000 years on earth, and

1,000 years on earth is the equivalent of one day with the space travelers. But God isn't limited as we are to one time framework or the other. The thing that is so mysterious is how God can move *through both frameworks at once.*

We can carry this relativistic time travel idea even further. Imagine a trip to the nearest galaxy, the Andromeda Galaxy, a round-trip of approximately 5,000,000 light-years. Even this would be feasible if a ship could move a little closer to the velocity of light than in the previous two examples. When the voyagers returned in a matter of years or even months, the earth would be about 3,000,000 years older!

But what if the ship could actually travel *at* the velocity of light? *Theoretically, time would stand still.* The smallest moment of time for the travelers could be the equivalent of billions of years in the universe. No one really knows what would happen in this case because even relativistic physics may not be sufficient for this. But the implications of such an idea for time, teleportation, and the universe are astounding.

The idea of man traveling at such high speeds isn't as far fetched as many would think. Reid shows that "if man continues increasing the speed at which he can travel at the same rate as in the past, he will be able to reach the speed of light by the year 2018."[5]

What would happen if a material object could move *faster* than light? Many say that time would run backward, making time trips into the past possible. But the idea of going faster than light is a real problem because, according to relativity, "no material object can move with a speed that equals or exceeds the speed of light."[6] One of the reasons for this is that the inertial mass of moving objects increases with speed and would become infinite at the speed of light.[7] But this doesn't mean that things having no mass couldn't exceed this barrier (what would be the "speed" of thought or prayer?).

Some scientists, for example, think that since neutrinos may have no physical properties they may move in their own "time" and possibly even faster than the speed of light.

One final thing about time and physics. Time isn't only affected by speed; it's also affected by matter. Einstein's general theory of relativity says in effect that matter produces gravitational fields that in turn affect the properties of space and time. Time intervals vary with the gravitational field, so that a clock on the sun would run slightly slower than a clock on earth.

Gravitational fields can even have the effect of *curving* space-time (we'll talk about the idea of the curvature of space-time in the next chapter). We can see from this overview of time and physics that the universe we live in is amazingly strange and complicated. All scientists (whether they admit it or not) must exercise faith in believing many things about this creation that are beyond comprehension.[8]

On the other hand, we should remember that the traditional conception of time is still good enough for *most purposes.* Our God-given comprehension of time is very workable. In spite of relativity, the concept of a simultaneous now has meaning to everyone (including Einstein).

Time and Precognition

As we've seen, no matter how much we examine time we can't really pin it down or keep it clearly in view. It's always there, but no one can grasp it. This is why we shouldn't be too hasty to accept conventional views of time.

One such view is that whatever is not *now* (that is, the past and the future) doesn't exist. Because we see reality in a progressive sequence of nows, we assume that everything is real only when it is now. There are some reasons to modify this standard notion. One reason is that this isn't the way God sees time (we'll talk about this shortly). Another reason is the wealth of documented cases of precognition (the ability to see beforehand things that haven't happened yet).

It appears that most precognitive dreams have little or nothing to do with the supernatural. Also, such dreams are more common than most people realize. These dreams are almost always vivid, and some of them keep recurring until they are fulfilled. Many of them involve glimpses of trivial events, and most of the rest go to the other extreme, depicting terrible accidents or tragedies. They're often brushed aside in spite of their vividness until they actually come true (usually a short time after the dream).

In some cases, these dreams depict a future that cannot be changed. Even when a person suddenly realizes an event in his dream is about to happen, he can do nothing to prevent it.

But in other cases, the future as seen in the dream *can* be changed because of the memory of the dream. For example, a man dreamed that he knocked down a boy with his car. Not long afterward he realized as he was driving that he was in the identical situation in his dream. He knew a boy would suddenly appear in the road, so he tried to ready himself to avoid him. Then the boy appeared (the same face as in the dream), but the driver was just able to miss him because he had been prepared by the memory of the dream.

In a similar dream, a woman was able to avoid the drowning of her baby in a creek because she remembered a detailed precognitive dream that showed her what would happen under the identical circumstances. In cases like these, the future can be seen and changed. Because it can be seen, it's not really non-existent, but because it can be changed it's not solidly there. In *Man and Time*, J. B. Priestly calls this "a half-made future," but this in no way would minimize God's sovereignty over creation.[9]

Montgomery suggests that such examples of precognition and ESP (extrasensory perception) represent a natural faculty that is "no more 'demonic,' (or 'angelic'!) than a faculty of lightning calculation or the ability to play the piano by ear."[10] It appears that the future somehow exists even though we haven't yet experienced it.

But how are people sometimes able to look through the veil that separates the future from the present? To explain this, different writers have proposed a second or even a third time dimension. To avoid confusion, Priestly calls these dimensions Time One, Time Two, and Time Three.[11] Time One involves our normal experience of a linear past, present, and future. But our minds can't be completely contained by Time One (consider ESP, precognition, and déjà vu). So Time Two (the time of our dreams) is needed. But even Time Two doesn't explain how people can sometimes change the possibilities revealed in Time Two (the man avoiding the boy, the woman preventing the drowning of her baby). This brings in Time Three, which contains all the alternative possibilities.

It is possible then, that time, like space, may be multidimensional. We just don't know. The only thing we can say with much certainty is that our conventional idea of time is inadequate. There's so much we don't know.

If the future and the past exist, they must exist in another kind of time (Time Two or Three). We couldn't travel into the past because we don't belong there. We didn't belong to Time One before we were born, and we don't belong even to our own past as we are now. Nevertheless, it's possible to go into the past or future in the nonchronological times Two or Three (Time One is chronological time). A good example of this is the revelation of future things that the apostle John received (the book of Revelation). John saw the future "in the Spirit" (Rev. 1:10). He was actively there, but not in the ordinary Time One sense. John's revelation covers more than a thousand years of the future (see Rev. 20:4–7, 10–15).

TIME AND GOD

How does God relate to time according to the Bible? In this area, as in so many others, the Bible is far ahead of us. This shouldn't be surprising since it's the revelation of the One who created this whole space-time universe. God's relation to time as seen in the Bible is far removed from any conventional view of time. For instance, Moses pictures this whole creation as only a brief period in God's eyes (Ps. 90:2–6). "For a thousand years in your sight are like a day that has just gone by, or like a watch in the night" (v. 4). This verse is interesting because it equates a period of time in God's sight with more than one period of man's time: "a day that has just gone by" (twelve hours) and "a watch in the night" (three hours).

It's impossible to describe fully God's eternality. We can only approach this by means of negatives. Ryrie writes, "God is not bound by the limitations of finitude and he is not bound by the succession of events, which is a necessary part of time."[12] There's only one biblical answer to the old question, "Where did God come from?" The answer is simply that God *always* was and is. He is the ultimate origin of everything we can sense. Time itself is a part of his creation.[13]

Peter tells us more about God's relation to time: "With the Lord a day is like a thousand years, and a thousand years are like a day" (2 Peter 3:8). God moves in many time frames at once. We can extend the concept in this verse by saying that a picosecond (trillionth of a second) to God is as a trillion years and a trillion years as one picosecond.

The ultimate extension is to say that with the Lord an infinitesimal moment is as an eternity, and eternity is as an infinitesimal moment. In some incomprehensible way *God sees each moment as an eternity and yet eternity as a moment.* God is in the *eternal Now*; he is timeless. This is why he revealed himself to Moses as "I AM WHO I AM" (Ex. 3:14). And Jesus said, "I tell you the truth … before Abraham was born, I am!" (John 8:58; see 8:24, 28; 18:6; Heb. 13:8).

In God's multidimensional eternity, the end is like the beginning. He inhabits all pasts and futures, and he is in all nows. "In one unified present glance he comprehends all things from everlasting, and the flutter of a seraph's wing a thousand ages hence is seen by him now without moving his eyes."[14] Only God can survey time in its entire extension.

God alone is outside of space and time; he created both when he made the universe. All God's creatures must exist in space and time. As we'll see, there's a qualitative difference between eternity as applied to God and to resurrected man. God's eternity isn't simply beginningless and endless time.

Some have argued that if God is not bound as humans are to the conditions of time, there's no way to make meaningful statements about him. One answer to this important objection is that space and time are real to God even though he's not limited to them. God has clearly communicated in space and in time. His clearest revelation was the incarnation of his Son. Christ subjected himself not only to death but also to the human bondage of space and time. God is immanent in space and time, and he is able to see the succession of events in the same way we do. The difference is that he's not bound by that succession.

God is the Lord of time. He is "the King eternal, immortal, invisible" (1 Tim.1:17). "Jesus Christ is the same yesterday and today and forever" (Heb. 13:8). His "origins are from old, from ancient times" (Mic. 5:2). He is "the Alpha and the Omega, the First and the Last, the Beginning and the End" (Rev. 22:13; see 1:8, 17; 2:8; 21:6; Isa. 44:6).

Not only can God see the length of the ages and the greatness of their duration, but he can also see things afar off as imminent—for instance, the New Testament teaching on the imminence of Christ's return (see Phil. 3:20; 1 Thess. 1:10; James 5:8; 2 Peter 3:8–13; 1 John 2:28; 3:2–3, even though these were written about 1,900 years ago). "Lord, you have been our dwelling place throughout all generations. Before the mountains were born or you brought forth the earth and the world, from everlasting to everlasting you are God" (Ps. 90:1–2).

TIME AND OTHER MYSTERIES

As we've said before, all biblical mysteries ultimately relate together since God is the Creator of all things. The time mystery, like the others, is only a problem when we try to limit God to our own ideas.

A close connection exists between the time and divine sovereignty/human responsibility mysteries. It can be illustrated by Martin Gardner's problem: "Is freedom of will no more than an illusion as the current of existence propels us into a future that in some unknown sense already exists? To vary the metaphor, is history a prerecorded motion picture, projected on the four-dimensional screen of our space-time for the amusement or edification of some unimaginable Audience?"[15]

This approach is inadequate because it limits God to our own perspective of one-dimensional linear time. We need to remember that God is outside time as we know it; he created time. Things like divine purpose, election, foreknowledge, and predestination are not temporal. They are eternal. Man can set up only a logical, not a chronological, relationship between these things. These are all part of the *timeless* decree of God. In God's mind *there never was another plan.*

Furthermore, God's plan includes *genuine* free will for men. C. S. Lewis develops this point nicely:

> Time is probably (like perspective) the mode of our perception. There's therefore in reality no question of God's at one point in time (the movement of creation) adapting the material history of the universe in advance to free acts which you or I are to perform at a later point in Time. To him all the physical events and all the human acts are present in an eternal Now. The liberation of finite wills and the creation of the whole material history of the universe (related to the acts of those wills in all the necessary complexity) is to him a single operation. In this sense God did not create the universe long ago but creates it at this minute—at every minute.[16]

There is perfect correlation of God's timeless eternal purpose with its temporal performance. "Everything which takes place in time corresponds exactly to what God purposed in eternity."[17]

The time mystery also relates to the Trinity and God-man mysteries. For instance, there is the timeless relationship between the Father and the Son that has been called "the eternal generation of the Son." There is also the mystery of how the Lord could bind himself to his own created time when he became the incarnated God-man.

TIME AND HISTORY

As we've seen, the Bible reveals that God's relation to time is very different from our own. Unlike God, we're subject to linear time that flows in one direction (Time One). The sum of all our nows makes up history. Lewis said that every sentence of history is labeled *Now*, and history must be read sentence by sentence. He spoke of "the holy present" because of the presence of God in every Now.[18] Time and history are very real to God since they're part of his creation. This is why all biblical events are tied into space-time history.

But from a *naturalistic* point of view, time seems to be running in endless cycles. This is the perspective Solomon temporarily takes: "Generations come and generations go.... The sun rises and the sun sets, and hurries back to where it rises.... All things are wearisome, more than one can say.... Is there anything of which one can say, 'Look! This is something new'? It was here already, long ago; it was here before our time" (Eccl. 1:4, 5, 8, 10).

This is precisely the outlook adopted by the Greeks. They thought of time as endlessly moving in a circle. To them time was an enslavement, a curse. Thus, their view of redemption was freedom from this endless circle of time. The New Testament proclamation that God has redeemed man in space and in time was therefore unthinkable to many Greeks.

The religious philosophies of India also developed this idea of cyclic cosmological time. Hinduism carried this out on a terrifying scale. It speaks of a cycle of four ages (Yugas) of decreasing length and virtue.[19] This cycle takes 4,320,000 years, and when it's complete, it will be followed by another cycle. One thousand of these cycles equals a day of Brahma, and another thousand makes a night of Brahma. One Brahma lives 100 years, so this works out to 300 trillion years. The process never stops. In this picture, life and history are ultimately futile and meaningless.

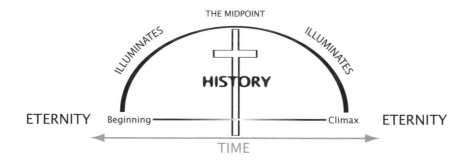

The biblical view of time and history is in direct contrast to these Greek and Indian concepts of cyclic ages. The Lord has revealed that history is actually moving in a straight line from a beginning to an end. The center of linear time is the resurrection of Jesus Christ. God's program of redemption is connected to a continuous time process that's heading toward a definite climax in history when Christ returns.

TIME AND ETERNITY

"He has made everything beautiful in its time. He has also set eternity in the hearts of men" (Eccl. 3:11). Though many have tried to repress it, people have a longing for eternity deep in their hearts. This longing often surfaces in fantasy literature. Tolkien's *The Lord of the Rings*, for example, is imbued with a subtle sadness because of the progressive conquest of profane time over sacred time (eternity) in Middle-earth. There are frequent references in this trilogy to the timeless paradise that has all but disappeared. Only a few snatches remain (for instance, Bilbo's comment about Rivendell: "Time does not seem to pass here: it just is").[20] Charles Williams and C. S. Lewis also worked with the idea of time and eternity. Lewis's Narnia has its own time, very different from that on earth. People could spend many years in Narnia only to discover on returning back to earth that no time had passed at all here.[21]

The desire for eternity is also reflected in efforts of many people to transcend space and time through mystical and drug experiences.

What does the Bible say about eternity? Is it simply endless time, or is it timelessness? Cullmann correctly argues that eternity *for man* isn't a state of timelessness.[22] He points out that the New Testament describes a future *in time* for man. Time won't cease, but it will go on and on in such a way that only God will be able to see the entire infinite succession of periods (see Eccl. 3:11b). Time is a part of God's creation, and creatures must live in it.

Nevertheless, there will still be some kind of qualitative change between time and eternity. For one thing, we may exist in a different *kind* of time. The one-dimensional line of time that we now normally experience may in eternity be like a plane or a solid. This brings us back to the idea of multiple dimensions of space and of time.

Another qualitative change between time and eternity will relate to our *experience of time* in our resurrected bodies. We'll have a different taste of time and new quality of life. Time will no longer be able to slowly suck the life out of us. Neither will we experience time as a constantly limiting burden. In this life, time is like a steadily moving river that carries our lives away; in the next life, it will be like a pool in which we'll luxuriate and create.

We need to keep in mind that the eternity we've been describing is creaturely eternity, not divine eternity. Cullmann fails to distinguish the two, and this results in his idea that God himself is bound by the linear succession of moments we know as time.[23] But God's eternity is "absolute, divine, complete, while that of man is partial and derivative."[24] God isn't time's servant; he is its Master.

Our experience of the new time of heaven is beyond our present ability to imagine. There will be no particular ages in heaven since the physical aging process will cease. It's possible that experience of duration will be brought closer to God's perspective. For instance, men like Paul and Peter who are present with the Lord may be experiencing this long interval between death and resurrection as only a few moments.

SOME IMPLICATIONS FOR EVERYDAY LIFE

The most important application of this study of time is our need to *develop an eternal perspective*. We must begin to look at our lives as God sees them, and consider the implications our small allotments of time have for eternity. Most people foolishly act as though they will never die. Moses knew better. During the thirty-eight years the children of Israel wandered aimlessly in the wilderness, an average of almost ninety people died per day. This led Moses to contrast the shortness of man's life with God's eternality (Ps. 90:1–6). God is everlasting, but man is like the grass that sprouts, then fades away.

Because most people don't have an eternal perspective, their values are reversed. Refusing to face questions about eternity, they're hurrying as quickly as they can to oblivion, stopping on their way to build monuments that crumble and are soon forgotten. People are preoccupied with the false god of "success" because they haven't learned the wisdom of laying up for themselves "treasures in heaven, where moth and rust do not destroy, and where thieves do not break in and steal" (Matt. 6:20). They don't realize there's much more to time than the mere chronological time we now experience (Time One).

Ultimate meaning can only come from seeing all things from God's perspective. There should be a sense of seriousness and responsibility in light of life's eternal consequences.

An eternal perspective is also of great value when suffering: "For our light and momentary troubles are achieving for us an eternal glory that far outweighs them all. So we fix our eyes not on what is seen, but on what is unseen. For what is seen is temporary, but what is unseen is eternal" (2 Cor. 4:17–18; see Rom. 8:18).

Christians need to be *controlled by the Holy Spirit in the realm of time.* The Scriptures clearly relate the proper use of time to *wisdom.* "Be very careful, then, how you live—not as unwise but as wise, making the most of every opportunity, because the days are evil. Therefore do not be foolish, but understand what the Lord's will is" (Eph. 5:15–17). It is always wise, for instance, to obey the Lord *at once.*

The Bible places a premium on *living daily with God.* It tells us to focus our attention on the present. "Therefore do not worry about tomorrow, for tomorrow will worry about itself. Each day has enough trouble of its own" (Matt. 6:34; see 2 Cor. 6:2). The only reality we have is *now.* It's always the now that directly relates to eternity.

This is why it's important for us to *appreciate and enjoy the process of things.* We tend to focus too much on product and not enough on process. Even heaven is a process, not a product. It is a *higher* process filled with perpetual activity without frustration and with complete fulfillment.

Plans and goals can be overemphasized, forcing people to lose appreciation for the present that we're always in. Besides, no one can be sure that (1) he will live long enough to reach his goal, and (2) he will know how to enjoy it if he does attain it.

James recognized the danger of placing plans before daily obedience to God's will. "Now listen, you who say, 'Today or tomorrow we will go to this or that city, spend a year there, carry on business and make money.' Why, you do not even know what will happen tomorrow. What is your life? You are a mist that appears for a little while and then vanishes. Instead, you ought to say, 'If it is the Lord's will, we will live and do this or that'" (4:13–15; see 1:10–11). There is no question that plans and goals are needed. In fact, one reason the average person doesn't accomplish very much is that he doesn't plan to. But plans and goals must be placed in the right perspective in submission to God's will.

Time is so valuable that it must be invested well, not wasted (Prov. 20:13; Eph. 5:15–17). It must be purchased and appropriated, but it can't be hoarded. When it's lost, it's irretrievable. Thus we need to structure time to use it best. This calls for personal discipline. A good, flexible, tailor-made schedule can lead to a strategic use of time.

We also need to *develop a sense of urgency* (see Rom. 13:11–12; 1 Peter 4:7) because "the Lord's coming is near" (James 5:8). However, we should take care not to become anxious about time. Remember that Christ was never in a hurry to do God's will. *God has given each of us enough time on this earth to carry out his will for our lives.* At the end of his ministry, Christ was able to say, "I have brought you glory on earth by completing the work you gave me to do" (John 17:4; see 2 Tim. 4:7). There's no need for a Christian to feel hemmed in by time's limitations. Consider these words of A. W. Tozer:

> The days of the years of our lives are few, and swifter than a weaver's shuttle. Life is a short and fevered rehearsal for a concert we cannot stay to give. Just when we appear to have attained some proficiency we are forced to lay our instruments down. There is simply not time enough to think, to become, to perform what the constitution of our natures indicates we are capable of.
>
> How completely satisfying to turn from our limitations to a God who has none. Eternal years lie in his heart. For him time doesn't pass, it remains; and those who are in Christ share with him all the riches of limitless time and endless years. God never hurries. There are no deadlines against which he must work. Only to know this is to quiet our spirits and relax our nerves.[25]

We'll be able to abide with the everlasting God forever in a new quality of existence that knows no frustration or boredom. Imagine the things you could accomplish with 10,000 years in a resurrected body that doesn't fatigue and requires no food or sleep! But as the familiar last stanza of "Amazing Grace" says, the 10,000 years is no time at all compared to eternity:

When we've been there 10,000 years,
Bright shining as the sun,
We've no less days to sing God's praise
Than when we first begun.

The LORD reigns, he is robed in majesty;
the LORD is robed in majesty
and is armed with strength.
The world is firmly established;
it cannot be moved.
Your throne was established long ago;
you are from all eternity. (Ps. 93:1–2)

Show me, O LORD, my life's end
and the number of my days;
let me know how fleeting is my life. (Ps. 39:4)

Teach us to number our days aright,
that we may gain a heart of wisdom. (Ps. 90:12)

Consider it pure joy, my brothers, whenever you face trials of many
kinds, because you know that the testing of your faith develops perseverance. Perseverance must finish its work so that you may be
mature and complete, not lacking anything. If any of you lacks wisdom, he should ask God, who gives generously to all without
finding fault, and it will be given to him. (James 1:2–5)

So we make it our goal to please him, whether we are at home in the
body or away from it. For we must all appear before the judgment seat
of Christ, that each one may receive what is due him for the things
done while in the body, whether good or bad. (2 Cor. 5:9–10)

Thirty Years Later

•   There has been, of course, a vast wealth of new discoveries and
    scientific knowledge in the past thirty years in fields from quan-
    tum physics to molecular biology to cosmology. In light of this,
    the section on time and physics would need substantial revision

if I were writing it today. For instance, in 1998, evidence for nonzero neutrino mass was reported. Yet in many ways, these advances strengthen and support the thesis of this chapter.

- The quote that "if man continues increasing the speed at which he can travel at the same rate as in the past, he will be able to reach the speed of light by the year 2018" would need revision, since the rate of progress hasn't been uniform.

- Advances in computer chips, with their exponential growth in speed and capacity, are also relevant to our perception of time.

- String theory proposes a second dimension of time in addition to five or six additional dimensions of space (in the case of superstring and M-theories). The standard model of particle physics is based on zero-dimensional points (particles), but string theory is built on one-dimensional extended objects (strings). These six to seven additional dimensions would be "compactified" by looping back upon themselves in the strings, so that they would not be detectable. Even so, the implications of a second dimension in time are intriguing. However, it would be a mistake to suppose that this form of multidimensionality opens the door to a spiritual dimension.

- It is not incoherent to affirm both the timelessness of the Eternal Now and his manifold actions in human history. As Boethius observed (*Consolation of Philosophy*, Book V), believing that God cannot perceive our future acts confuses the simultaneous eternal presence of God and his perspective with the projection of our own finite experience of events across the progression of time. Orthodox writers distinguish the essence of God and the energies of God; in his essence, he is timeless, but in his energies, he manifests himself and works within time.

- The Greek word *chronos* refers to the ordinary kind of time that can be measured by clocks and other chronometers. Another Greek word for time is *kairos*, and this relates to opportunity. "Therefore be careful how you walk, not as unwise men but as wise, making the most of your time [*kairon*], because the days are evil" (Eph. 5:15–16 NASB). "Conduct yourselves with wisdom toward outsiders, making the most of the opportunity [*kairon*]" (Col. 4:5 NASB). *Chronos* is the ordinary time we plan in our calendars; *kairos* is opportunity time, and we can't plan for it, since we never know when it will come. God orchestrates special opportunities in our lives, and we can easily overlook them by misconstruing them as interruptions. The most significant thing we do today probably won't be in our planner; instead, it will be our response to a divinely appointed opportunity or "*kairos* moment" (e.g., a chance encounter, a strong impression to call or pray for someone, or an unforeseen act of service). Instead of managing our time tightly to accomplish objectives, we would do well to manage our time loosely enough to enhance relationships. Jesus' life was full of these moments.

- Truth in science or any other discipline is never determined by a majority vote; the history of science is strewn with discarded theories that were once held by the majority. Some scientists argue it would be a mistake to assume too dogmatically that current theories won't need to be substantially revised or discarded. This minority movement claims there are serious flaws in general relativity (equivalence of gravity and acceleration), special relativity (the speed of light as an unchanging constant), matter-energy interconversion, Heisenberg's uncertainty principle, and current cosmological theories (particularly warped space, Hawking's unified concepts, the big bang, etc.), since they violate the first and second laws of thermodynamics, Maxwell's equations of electromagnetism, and many of the other well-established laws of science.

Chapter 8

SPACE

(The Creation)

G od's creation, though temporarily fallen, is exquisite and mysterious. It's filled with mind-boggling phenomena that defy comprehension and description. The more science is able to examine the real nature of things, the more perplexing they become. As we probe into the universe, we become increasingly aware that we know almost nothing at all. The horizon keeps getting more distant as we climb higher.

Even the things we do "understand" are treasure-houses of unlimited information. We are only beginning to realize how subtle and intricate creation is. Upon examination, a tiny object such as a drop of water can turn into a little universe that can be endlessly explored. And a single living cell is more complex and wonderful than all the machines man ever made.

This chapter will describe some of the strange qualities of space and consider whether the universe is finite or infinite. Against this background, it will explore the biblical teaching on God's relation to space, for this is another mystery.

SPACE AND PHYSICS

Space is bound up with time in a continuum, which seems to extend from the infinitesimal toward the infinite. Scientists have thus far been unable to detect a definite limitation in either direction.

Let's look first at submicroscopic space. At this level, particles, atoms, and molecules are in continuous violent motion. Heisenberg's uncertainty principle states that the elementary particles that constitute all matter are *blurs* that can't be focused in space and time. An elementary particle's position or linear momentum can be known, but both cannot be known simultaneously.[1] It is impossible to visually conceive what these elementary particles are really like, yet everything we touch is made of them.

But there's more. These particles aren't *things* at all. Like light, they behave not only as particles with mass but also as *waves*. This is another natural mystery, because they're two completely different entities at once. It's meaningless to discuss how much room an electron or proton takes up since they aren't solid spheres of matter. An electron can even occupy *two places at the same time!*

Everything is made of atoms that in turn are reducible to almost completely empty space. Electrons are constantly whirling around the nuclei of atoms at such great distances that if the nucleus of an atom were magnified to one inch in size, the electrons would be more than a mile and a half away. All the rest is empty space.

On further examination, even electrons and the particles that make up the nucleus turn into waves. So the atom is a practically empty system of superimposed waves. Barnett concludes that "all matter is made of waves and we live in a world of waves."[2]

If this isn't strange enough, we can go one more step—transmuting concrete into the abstract. If the particles that make up matter are wave patterns, what is the medium that carries the waves? Since the waves are movements, what is it that moves? "Short of calling it the grin of the Cheshire Cat, it was named the 'psi field' or 'psi function.'"[3] This is a completely abstract and nonmaterial field, yet it supports all material things.

The traditional concept of matter is no longer valid. Things that seem solid are really made of pure activity. Matter reduces to energy, and energy to undulations of the unknown. Thus, we live in a world of impossibilities and in a universe that's more fantastic than we can hope to imagine.

As we move from submicroscopic space to our own intermediate order of size, things appear to be back under control. Because of the law of large numbers, when trillions of atoms form visible objects, the atoms' wild deviations cancel out each other, so larger objects are highly predictable and can be locked into space and time.

But we need to remember that the world of our experiences is really a small raft floating on the wavy sea of the infinitesimal under the mysterious sky of the terrifyingly large. And even our world of tons and miles is constantly bombarded by forms of energy that emanate from the realms of the small and the great. Cosmic rays, X-rays, radio waves, and most waves from radioactive materials continually stream through our bodies as though we were phantoms. Forms of energy wholly unknown to us are passing through space, still transparent to our most sensitive receivers.

Now we turn to cosmic space, the space of the distant stars and galaxies. Newton believed in absolute space and absolute motion, holding that space, like time, is an infinitely large thing that never changes. This concept was challenged by thinkers like Leibniz and, more recently, by the relativistic physics of Einstein. It now appears that space can be affected by the same things that distort time: velocity and gravitation.

At velocities very close to that of light, space actually begins to contract. George Gamow wrote, "If we can imagine objects moving with speeds 50, 90, and 99 percent of light speed, their lengths will be reduced respectively to 86, 45, and 14 percent of their sizes when standing on the ground."[4] Objects shrink in the direction of their own motion, but this contraction is negligible until extraordinary speeds are reached.

Space can be distorted by strong gravitational fields as well as extreme speed. Einstein's gravitational laws point to the idea that space-time is a flexible and plastic continuum. Stars, clusters, galaxies, and supergalaxies produce interlocking patterns of powerful gravitational fields. These fields determine the properties of the space (and time) around them. "Wherever there is matter and motion, the continuum is disturbed. Just as a fish swimming in the sea agitates the water around it, so a star, a comet, or a galaxy distorts the geometry of the space-time through which it moves."[5]

There aren't absolute standards in the natural creation. Space is nothing apart from the arrangement of the objects that occupy it. The space-time continuum is determined by gravitational fields; gravitational fields are produced by matter; matter is reducible to waves of energy; and energy consists of sheer, indefinable activity—a very abstract concept.

Motion, too, is relative, and there are no absolutes in nature by which it can be measured. No one knows (or could know) of a point in the universe that doesn't move at all.

We said before that submicroscopic space is relatively empty. The "material" in an atom takes up less than one-trillionth of the atom's volume. Cosmic space is also nearly empty. Even in densely packed stellar clusters the stars are so far away from each other that there's practically no chance that two of them will collide.

However, the density of stars themselves ranges from near vacuum (red giants) to unbelievable densities (white dwarfs and neutron stars). The density of a neutron star, for instance, is about *a billion tons per cubic inch*.[6] This is so dense that steel is almost a vacuum in comparison.

Far greater densities exist in black holes. These are invisible since their gravities are so great that even light cannot escape from the star. The star has been crushed to tiny volume and unimaginable density.

THE ORIGIN OF SPACE

Scientists greatly disagree as to how the universe started. One theory of the origin of the universe holds that it had no beginning and that matter is eternal. A variation of this is the steady state theory, which proposes that matter is being constantly created near the center of the universe and destroyed at the outer perimeter of space. There are several difficulties with this theory. Two of them are (1) there's not enough evidence to support it, and (2) it violates the law of conservation of mass and energy.

The big bang theory is currently the most popular. It states that the universe was *suddenly created* 10 to 20 billion years ago. A great glob of super-dense energy violently exploded the moment it came into being. This produced hot gas clouds that formed into galaxies and other celestial bodies. These bodies continue to grow more distant from one another as the universe keeps expanding due to the initial big bang.

There are two variations of the big bang theory. One is that gravitational pull may eventually stop the galaxies' expansion and cause them to rush inward, eventually to form a new glob of super-dense energy. In this case a new "big bang" would occur, and the process would start over. Each complete cycle would take, according to some estimates, about 80 billion years. But even with this "pulsating universe" idea, the process couldn't last forever. Each successive bang would have less available energy unless new energy was formed out of nothing. Another problem with this view is that there doesn't seem to be enough mass to produce the gravitational pull necessary to cause the galaxies to stop expanding.

The other variation of the big bang theory is that the universe will continue to expand forever. This variation seems to be more consistent with the cosmological implications of the second law of thermodynamics. The overall tendency in all processes is away from concentration of energy and high temperature. Energy is becoming less and less usable, and the disorder (entropy) of the universe is increasing. In other words, the universe eventually will die a cold, vacant, dark, and vast death.

Those who trace this process backward argue that the universe has not always existed./ Otherwise, it would have run down long ago, and no one would be alive today to speak about it.

All humanly devised theories of the universe's origin, including the big bang theory, are inadequate. The big bang theory may admit that the universe was suddenly created a finite time ago, but it still leaves unanswered the most important question of all: Where did the initial matter, energy, space, and time come from?

People without God are constantly trying to answer the old philosophical questions with systems that rule out the supernatural. But all theories that limit themselves to the four-dimensional space-time continuum fall pitifully short of explaining the origin and destiny of the universe and the origin of life. Neither can they explain the complexity of the universe and the personality of man. The God of the Bible provides a meaningful basis for order, life, and intelligence. The Scriptures teach that the orderly universe came from the uncreated, omnipresent, omnipotent God of order; complex living systems came from the living God; the human mind came from God's omniscient mind; personhood came from the personal, loving God; and morality came from the holy and infinitely good God.

Apart from a revelation from the infinite-personal God, there's no hope of finding answers. But God *has* revealed himself to us in the Bible, and he tells us that he is the Author of all things. "Creation of a universe out of nothing is infinitely beyond anything and everything but an omniscient and omnipotent God."[8]

THE SIZE OF THE UNIVERSE

The human mind can't really comprehend either the microcosmos or the macrocosmos. Cosmic space is too vast for any of us to grasp. The best we can do to picture the greatness and the smallness of space is to use our intuition and work with analogies.

There's no question that the universe's immensity is terrifying. But the big question that's still being debated is whether space is finite or infinite. Many scientific supporters can be found for either position, and a great number of others say we simply don't know.

It was hoped that the question could be settled by counting the number of galaxies—if this number increases more slowly than the cube of the distance, space is closed and finite; if it increases more rapidly, space is open and infinite. Edwin Hubble made such a count and concluded that space is a closed sphere with a diameter of approximately 70 billion light-years. However, more recent investigations show that Hubble's figures must be revised due to uncertainty about the methods of determining the distances of these remote galaxies.[9] As far as the empirical evidence is concerned, we can't presently decide whether the universe is finite or infinite.

In any case, space can't really be comprehended. First, a finite, spherical model of the universe can't be visualized. If you try to picture a huge sphere, you have two problems: (1) The sphere itself isn't solid, and (2) the human mind can't conceive of a sphere that's *without space outside of the sphere*. In other words, the sphere of space seems to be surrounded by empty space. This is because our minds can't visualize anything apart from space and time.

Second, the infinite model of the universe is also incomprehensible for two reasons: (1) none of us can envision infinite space; and (2) if the universe is infinite, yet another mystery would be introduced—the universe is spatially infinite yet finite with respect to God since it is part of his creation.

The Bible doesn't resolve whether space is finite or infinite in the normal three-dimensional sense. It only tells us that, relative to God's absolute infinitude, space is quite limited and even insignificant.

The study of astronomy can be very helpful in a spiritual sense. When people who study this field begin to grasp the terrible vastness of the cosmos in brief moments (it is a *feeling* as much as it is a visualization and can't be maintained for long), they can more effectively increase their appreciation of God's greater vastness. But the real mystery of space is that God is outside of space yet in space at the same time.

SPACE AND GOD

The Scriptures make it quite clear that God created everything there is by the word of his mouth. This includes space itself. "It is I who made the earth and created mankind upon it. My own hands stretched out the heavens; I marshaled their starry hosts" (Isa. 45:12). "By wisdom the LORD laid the earth's foundations, by understanding he set the heavens in place" (Prov. 3:19; see Prov. 8:22–31; Jer. 10:12).

God "calls things that are not as though they were" (Rom. 4:17). He *spoke* the universe into existence. "By the word of the LORD were the heavens made, their starry host by the breath of his mouth.... For he spoke, and it came to be; he commanded, and it stood firm" (Ps. 33:6, 9; compare Gen. 1:3, 6, 9, 11, 14, 20, 24, 26).[10]

God is the Lord over space. He "created the heavens and stretched them out" (Isa. 42:5). He "made the Pleiades and Orion" (Amos 5:8) along with the myriads of other stars and "calls them each by name" (Isa. 40:26).

The biblical doctrine of creation is unique, because God created the universe *out of nothing*. There was no antecedent raw material that had always existed. Other creation accounts assume the prior existence of space, time, energy, and matter. Only the God of the Bible is big enough and personal enough to have created the complex universe and personal creatures like men and angels. It is a glorious and subtle creation even though it has been seriously marred by the effects of sin.

As science has only recently discovered, the visible things that God created are really made out of invisible components. "By faith we understand that the universe was formed at God's command, so that what is seen was not made out of what was visible" (Heb. 11:3).

God not only created the universe but also upholds every part of it. Jesus continuously is "sustaining all things by his powerful word" (Heb. 1:3). All things come *from* God the Father and *through* Jesus Christ (1 Cor. 8:6). Christ is "before all things, and in him all things hold together" (Col. 1:17). We owe our moment-to-moment existence to the Son of God.

God is therefore the author of the cosmos and not a character within it. Since he created space-time, it's pointless to try to find him among the stars. Could one find Handel himself by searching through the notes and words of his *Messiah*? But even though God is outside the dimensions of space and time as we know them, this does not prevent him from revealing himself to men in special ways and in space-time historical events. The clearest example, of course, is the incarnation of Christ.

The four-dimensional space-time continuum isn't sufficient to explain the origin of life and the universe. There must be something more. What is needed is another dimension beyond nature as we know it. This is a supernatural or spiritual dimension. God isn't just quantitatively bigger than the universe he created. His mode of existence is qualitatively different from that of the universe. The heavens and earth are dependent on God, but God is dependent on none but himself.

Since God is spirit (John 4:24), he is measureless. In the same way, his spirit creatures (angels) are in another dimension. So it's meaningless to talk about how "large" an angel (or even a soul or a spirit) is. Angels and demons are in a different kind of space that in some sense is all around our three-dimensional space. Spirit beings are "nearer" to us than most people think. Just as a three-dimensional creature wouldn't be visible to inhabitants of a two-dimensional world, so a being in four spatial dimensions would be invisible in our three-dimensional world.

Even angelic creatures must exist in some kind of space and time. They're not outside of space and time as God is, since they aren't omnipresent and they haven't always existed.

God alone is the Creator, and he is the only being who isn't limited to space. Yet he is in space in the sense that he is in all places at once. But all places cannot contain him: "Will God really dwell on earth? The heavens, even the highest heaven, cannot contain you. How much less this temple I have built!" (1 Kings 8:27) "This is what the LORD says: 'Heaven is my throne, and the earth is my footstool. Where is the house you will build for me? Where will my resting place be? Has not my hand made all these things, and so they came into being?'" (Isa. 66:1–2; see Acts 7:48–50; 17:24).

God is intimate with all his creation and he is Lord over everything he has made. He is "God in heaven above and on the earth below" (Josh. 2:11). God's relation to his universe is graphically depicted in Psalm 113:5–6: "Who is like the LORD our God, the One who sits enthroned on high, who stoops down to look on the heavens and the earth?"

The astronomy of the Bible is God centered, not man centered. While there are many biblical passages that acknowledge the immeasurable greatness of the universe with its innumerable stars, the Scriptures also emphasize that compared to God, space is nothing. Since God is the only absolute, size is relative. From God's perspective, there's really little difference between the size of the smallest microbe and the largest cluster of galaxies.

God has all power over his creation. He will, in fact, destroy this present cosmos and create another (see 2 Peter 3:10 13). "Behold, I will create new heavens and a new earth. The former things will not be remembered, nor will they come to mind" (Isa. 65:17; compare Isa. 66:22 and Rev. 21:1). The new universe will be better and more glorious than the present one (Rev. 22:3–5).

HEAVEN AND HELL

Many people have scoffed at the Scriptures because the Bible speaks about the existence of heaven and hell. The current worldview is that science has somehow proved that heaven and hell can't exist, but this is far from the truth. We've already seen how the views of modern science in this area are inadequate because they don't explain the existence of the universe. The mysteries of the universe point to a realm beyond nature itself, a supernatural dimension.

Heaven is neither "near" nor "far" in the ordinary three-dimensional sense of space. It can't be reached by traveling in any spaceship, even if the ship could travel at relativistic speeds. Heaven is indeed a place, but the word *place* in this context must take on a new meaning.[11]

Heaven has its own space and time in which its inhabitants subsist. It's distinct from the heavens of our universe. Paul calls it the "third heaven" (2 Cor. 12:2). The first heaven is our atmosphere and the second heaven is space, the realm of the stars. Solomon also draws a distinction between two kinds of heaven: "The heavens, even the highest heaven [literally, 'heaven of heavens'], cannot contain you" (1 Kings 8:27). This "highest heaven" is qualitatively different from the heaven of the stars. Since it may be in another dimension, it could in some way be all around us (see Acts 17:27–28). Again, this isn't to say that heaven is some kind of transcendent order beyond space and time, for only God can be outside of space and time in an absolute sense.

We've seen that God is planning to create a new heaven and a new earth. The nature of space, time, matter (for instance, transparent gold; Rev. 21:18), and energy will be different in this new universe. It will be imbued with the glory of God. Even God's throne will be "relocated" since the Holy City, the New Jerusalem, will come "down out of heaven from God" (Rev. 21:2, 10; see 22:3–4).

THE RELEVANCE OF THIS MYSTERY

The biblical concept of a God so great that space can't contain him has real significance for all people. Nearly three thousand years ago David wrote, "When I consider your heaven, the work of your fingers, the moon and the stars, which you have set in place, what is man that you are mindful of him, the son of man that you care for him?" (Ps. 8:3–4; see Ps. 144:3–4; Heb. 2:6). Job said almost the same thing: "What is man that you make so much of him, that you give him so much attention?" (7:17).

Man is nothing at all compared to the vastness of God's creation, yet he is significant in the Creator's eyes. One reason God created the splendors of the universe was to reveal his awesome power and glory to man (see Rom. 1:19–20). The arrogance and pride of so many people are utter foolishness in light of our Lilliputian planet and sun. Even our galaxy is only a speck among billions.

Only when we admit that we're nothing apart from God are we ready to respond to the life-giving offer of reconciliation that Christ provides.

The size of space and God's relation to space are beyond comprehension. The better we realize the vastness of the universe, the greater our conception of God must become.

To admit that there is one who lies beyond us, who exists outside of all our categories, who will not be dismissed with a name, who will not appear before the bar of our reason, nor submit to our curious inquiries: this requires a great deal of humility, more than most of us possess, so we save face by thinking God down to our level, or at least down to where we can manage him. Yet how he eludes us! For he is everywhere while he is nowhere, for "where" has to do with matter and space, and God is independent of both. He is unaffected by time or motion, is wholly self-dependent and owes nothing to the worlds his hands have made.[12]

But if the earth is so puny, why is God so concerned with all the affairs of our planet? The question that Job and David asked is a real problem because of our natural way of thinking. If you're in a carpeted room, look at the carpet and isolate one loop or strand from among the thousands of similar loops. Now imagine yourself devoting the remainder of your life to the study and analysis of this single loop of threads!

The analogy isn't too extreme because there are *far more* galaxies in the universe than there are loops in your carpet; and each galaxy contains, on the average, hundreds of billions of stars like our own sun. Yet God declares that we're of infinite value in his sight. Part of the problem of how this can be so is solved when we remember that sizes mean little to God. Even though the earth is a minute speck in the panorama of God's creation, it is on *this* planet that the central program of God's plan is happening.

If it seems incredible that God would center his plan on our planet, how much more incredible is it that he'd actually send his beloved Son to die in payment for our sins! Jesus Christ created this immense universe with all its hundreds of billions of galaxies and sextillions of stars, yet how he humbled himself.

> He was despised and rejected by men,
> a man of sorrows, and familiar with suffering.
> Like one from whom men hide their faces
> he was despised, and we esteemed him not.
> Surely he took up our infirmities
> and carried our sorrows. (Isa. 53:3–4)

The more we perceive the terrifying greatness of the universe, the more we can really begin to appreciate the shame and condescension Christ willingly bore. He loved us enough to become man and pay for our sins with his own blood. "He was in the world, and though *the world was made through him*, the world did not recognize him. He came to that which was his own, but his own did not receive him. Yet to all who received him, to those who believed in his name, he gave the right to become children of God" (John 1:10–12).

WITNESS OF THE WORLD AND THE WORD (PS. 19)
1.   The Meaning of the Skies (vv. 1–6): God's Grandeur
2.   The Message of the Scriptures (vv. 7–11): The Lord's Grace
3.   The Meditation of the Soul (vv. 12–14): The Redeemer's Guarantee

Meditate on Psalm 19 using this outline and these brief thoughts.[13]

> O LORD, our Lord,
> how majestic is your name in all the earth!
> You have set your glory
> above the heavens. (Ps. 8:1)
>
> Sing to the LORD, all the earth;
> proclaim his salvation day after day.
> Declare his glory among the nations,
> his marvelous deeds among all peoples.
> For great is the LORD and most worthy of praise;
> he is to be feared above all gods.
> For all the gods of the nations are idols,
> but the LORD made the heavens.
> Splendor and majesty are before him;
> strength and joy in his dwelling place. (1 Chron. 16:23–27)

Praise be to you, O LORD,
God of our father Israel,
from everlasting to everlasting.
Yours, O LORD, is the greatness and the power
and the glory and the majesty and the splendor,
for everything in heaven and earth is yours.
Yours, O LORD, is the kingdom;
you are exalted as head over all.
Wealth and honor come from you;
you are the ruler of all things.
In your hands are strength and power
to exalt and give strength to all.
Now, our God, we give you thanks,
and praise your glorious name. (1 Chron. 29:10–13)

Praise the LORD, O my soul.
O LORD my God, you are very great;
you are clothed with splendor and majesty.
He wraps himself with light as with a garment;
he stretches out the heavens like a tent. (Ps. 104:1–2)

Blessed be your glorious name, and may it be exalted above all blessing and praise. You alone are the LORD. You made the heavens, even
the highest heavens, and all their starry host, the earth and all that is
on it, the seas and all that is in them. You give life to everything, and
the multitudes of heaven worship you. (Neh. 9:5–6)

THIRTY YEARS LATER

- Just as the plethora of new scientific knowledge would require a
  substantial revision of the time and physics section in chapter 7,
  the same would be true of the space and physics section in this
  chapter. From quarks to quasars, many of the rules have changed.
- In the last three decades, scores of new fine-tuning restraints have
  been determined that provide evidence of the universe's fitness for
  life. The fundamental forces (the strong nuclear force, the weak
  nuclear force, the electromagnetic force, and the gravitational
  force) as well as the expansion rate of the universe are so finely
  tuned that extremely minute changes in them would render the

universe incapable of sustaining life. The same is also true on a galactic scale, as well as the scales of our solar system and of our earth. If the probabilities of only fifty of the more than two hundred (and rapidly growing) fine-tuning parameters are added, they yield an impossibly low probability for the existence of extraterrestrial life, even assuming 10^{20} planets in the cosmos. A conservative estimate of the probability of two hundred of these finely tuned parameters occurring by chance is 10^{215}. The only solution for avoiding the obvious implication that the universe was created with us in mind (the anthropic principle) is the claim that our universe is part of a multiverse and is only one of a virtually unlimited number of other universes. This scenario enables the skeptic to claim we just happen to be in one of the few just-right universes. This is related to the possible theoretical implications of superstring theory, M-theory, and brane cosmology (branes are multidimensional objects that are theorized to float in an eleven-dimensional space and contain universes). Notwithstanding the elegance of these theories, they have no empirical warrant and they also require violations of the first and second laws of thermodynamics, two of the most fundamental laws of physics. Thus, these multiuniverse speculations require enormous leaps of faith in an attempt to avoid the implication of design associated with the consistent empirical evidence that our universe had a beginning, before which there was no space and time.

- Inflationary theory, if correct, would indicate that the universe has a "flat" rather than positively or negatively curved geometry. But due to the stretching of space with its expansion after the big bang, astronomers now say that the universe is at least 156 billion light-years wide, even though it is 13.7 billion years old.

- Most astronomers now agree the universe will go on expanding forever. Indeed, recent observations have suggested that the expansion of the universe is accelerating over cosmic time due to the influence of an antigravity force called "dark energy." Fluctuations of the background radiation in the cosmos have led to the conclusion that the universe is 13.7 billion years old and that 23 percent of the cosmos consists of dark matter and 73 percent consists of dark energy. This would mean that only 4 percent of the cosmos consists of conventional matter.

- Current research indicates there appear to be structures in the universe that are larger than clusters and superclusters of galaxies.

These consist of vast volumes of space with few galaxies, surrounded by bubbles of clusters of galaxies. Computer simulations of the early universe also tend to indicate a clumping of matter along the surface of large shells.

- The recently estimated number of galaxies is more than 200 billion, and each galaxy contains up to 400 billion stars. The number of stars in the known universe is estimated to be 7×10^{22} (70 sextillion). This is more than all the grains of sand on all the beaches and deserts of the world.

- Along other scientific lines, the Intelligent Design (ID) movement has emerged in the last thirty years. Although critics claim that ID is merely old-line creationism in disguise, it's actually quite different in that it focuses on inference to the best explanation, and it argues that if the evidence doesn't support chance or necessity, the only other explanation is design. But ID says nothing about the source of the design and could be compatible with a wide variety of approaches, including theism, deism, panentheism, pantheism, and panspermia (the theory that life on Earth originated from outer space). Recent years have revealed a level of elegance, intricacy, beauty, synergy, fine-tuning, and complexity that is breathtaking and beyond anyone's wildest speculations only a few decades ago. The term "specified complexity" describes information, and the levels of information in complex bio-macromolecules is now known to be extraordinary. The amount of information in the human genome contained in the six feet of DNA within each human cell corresponds to more information than there is in a set of the *Encyclopaedia Britannica*. Typically those who resist such clear implications of Intelligent Design will justify their bias by confusing science (a method of empirical analysis) with scientism (a naturalistic, materialistic philosophy).

Chapter 9

SPACE

(Omnipresence versus Localization)

I n the last chapter we said that God is outside of space since it is a part of his creation, yet he is also in space at the same time. We said there's no way we can visualize either infinite space or finite space. Since we're creatures, we are locked into space and time, unable to comprehend God's unique relation to the space and time of his created universe.

Now we need to explore another facet of the space mystery: the revealed fact that God is omnipresent yet specially localized.

THE OMNIPRESENCE OF GOD

God's omnipresence is in itself a mystery. There's a sense in which the whole of God is in every place. God actually fills the heavens and the earth (Jer. 23:24). The heavens and the highest heavens belong to God (Deut. 10:14), but they cannot contain him (1 Kings 8:27; 2 Chron. 2:6). So God fills all spaces, but no space can contain him.

God's presence in more than one place is incomprehensible to the human mind. David, in a psalm about God's omniscience and omnipresence, declares that "such knowledge is too wonderful for me, too lofty for me to attain" (Ps. 139:6). He continues:

Where can I go from your Spirit?
Where can I flee from your presence?
If I go up to the heavens, you are there;
if I make my bed in the depths, you are there.
If I rise on the wings of the dawn,
if I settle on the far side of the sea,
even there your hand will guide me,
your right hand will hold me fast.

If I say, "Surely the darkness will hide me
and the light become night around me,"
even the darkness will not be dark to you;
the night will shine like the day,
for darkness is as light to you. (Ps. 139:7–12)

Since God is in all places, there's no hope of escaping from his complete presence. He is even in the depths (in Sheol, the abode of the dead, v. 8, NASB). "Though they dig down to the depths of the grave, from there my hand will take them. Though they climb up to the heavens, from there I will bring them down" (Amos 9:2). God's presence extends to all parts of the sea, the sky, and space. No one can avoid his presence, no matter how fast he is able to travel. He is "God in heaven above and on the earth below" (Josh. 2:11; also see Isa. 66:1–2; Acts 7:48–50).

All three members of the Godhead are omnipresent. The Father is omnipresent, and the Son "fills everything in every way" (Eph. 1:23). Christ declared that "where two or three come together in my name, there am I with them" (Matt. 18:20). He also said, "And surely I am with you always, to the very end of the age" (Matt. 28:20). Christ must be omnipresent to sustain all things by his powerful word (Heb. 1:3; see Col. 1:17). The Holy Spirit also is present everywhere ("Where can I go from your Spirit?" Ps. 139:7; see 1 Cor. 6:19; Eph. 2:22). All three persons are present in all places together as one God. There is no place where one is present without the other two being there as well.

In a real sense, the whole of God is present in every place. He is not diffused throughout his creation so that only a tiny part of him is in each place. Instead, "he is wholly present as fully as though he were nowhere else—Father, Son, and Spirit—in every human temple in which he dwells, and in every part of his dominion."[1] He is equally present in all places at all times. Augustine wrote:

> You fill the heaven and the earth. Do they therefore contain You? ... When heaven and earth are filled with You, into what do You pour that surplus of Yourself which remains over? Or is it not rather the case that You have no need to be contained by anything? ... You who fill everything are wholly present in everything which You fill. Or can we say that, because all things together are unable to contain You wholly, therefore each thing contains only a part of You? Does every thing contain the same part? Or are there different parts for different things in accordance with the varying sizes of the things? That would mean that some parts of You could be greater and some smaller than others. Shall we not rather say this: everywhere You are present in Your entirety, and no single thing can contain You in Your entirety?[2]

We must be careful to distinguish the doctrine of the divine presence from the error of pantheism. Pantheism fails to distinguish the created order from the Creator because it says that God is nature and nature is God.[3] On the other hand, the Bible teaches that though God is present everywhere, he is not resident in everything. God fills the heavens and the earth, but the things in the heavens and the earth shouldn't be called God. When you pick up a book or lean against a tree, you aren't touching God as the pantheist would assert.

The Bible says God is everywhere, but it also says he is separate from the things of the world. God is immanent within his creation but at the same time transcendent above it (see chapter 10).

There's no limit to God's presence, and no place is "closer" to God than any other place. Size and place mean little to God; they do not limit him at all. He doesn't need to travel, and he can act in all parts of the universe at once. As God exercises his attributes, all things are affected at the same time. "God is over all things, under all things; outside all; within but not enclosed; without but not excluded; above but not raised up; below but not depressed; wholly above, presiding; wholly beneath, sustaining; wholly within, filling."[4]

Because God is in all places, he is able to see all things at once. Using anthropomorphic language, he not only looks down at the sky; he also looks *up* at it at the same time. Unlike us, he can see all parts of three-dimensional objects equally well. Imagine, for instance, being able to see the entire surface of a two-foot globe at once. We could only do this by using mirrors or by projecting the globe on a two-dimensional surface (like a map).

THE LOCALIZED PRESENCE OF GOD

God is *completely* present in all places at once. Yet the Bible makes it equally clear that each member of the Trinity is also localized in specific places. The Lord can somehow manifest his presence in special ways. In some inexplicable manner there is a difference between God's omnipresence and his *manifest* presence.[5]

Let's look first at the specially localized presence of God the Father. The Scriptures teach that God's throne in heaven is the localized center of his dominion. Heaven is indeed a place, even though the language used to describe it is usually figurative and anthropomorphic (see chapter 8). The Father, Son, and Holy Spirit are there along with myriads of angels and a host of redeemed people (Heb. 12:22–23). But this place is qualitatively different from our ordinary concept of a place, operating perhaps in a spiritual (but very real) dimension with a space different from our own. Nevertheless, it constitutes a special localization of God. In fact, the places and things of earth are really only a shadow when they're compared with the deeper reality of heavenly things (Heb. 8:5; 9:23).

God's throne is mentioned in a number of Old and New Testament passages. Isaiah describes his vision of God: "In the year that King Uzziah died, I saw the Lord seated on a throne, high and exalted, and the train of his robe filled the temple" (6:1). God's manifest presence was so intense that Isaiah was instantly aware of his utter sinfulness before the Holy God (v. 5).

The apostle John also recorded his vision: "At once I was in the Spirit, and there before me was a throne in heaven with someone sitting on it. And the one who sat there had the appearance of jasper and carnelian. A rainbow, resembling an emerald, encircled the throne" (Rev. 4:2–3; other passages that mention heaven and God's throne are 1 Kings 22:19; 2 Chron. 18:18; Pss. 103:19; 123:1; Isa. 63:15; Heb. 8:1; 12:2; Rev. 5:13).

The glory of God's presence (the *shekinah*) is another example of his special localized presence. From the standpoint of God's omnipresence, Solomon knew that there was no way the temple he had just completed could contain God. "But will God really dwell on earth? The heavens, even the highest heaven, cannot contain you. How much less this temple I have built!" (1 Kings 8:27). God himself reiterated this same truth later (Isa. 66:1–2).

Yet from the standpoint of God's localized presence, he was actually able to dwell in the most holy place in the temple. The *shekinah* glory came and filled the house of the Lord. "The priests could not enter the temple of the LORD because the glory of the LORD filled it" (2 Chron. 7:2; also see 1 Kings 8:10–11). This glory of God's manifest presence later departed because of Israel's iniquity (Ezek. 10:3–4, 18–19; 11:22–23).

Jacob also encountered God's localized presence. At Bethel he had a vision of God in a dream. "When Jacob awoke from his sleep, he thought, 'Surely the LORD is in this place, and I was not aware of it.' He was afraid and said, 'How awesome is this place! This is none other than the house of God; this is the gate of heaven'" (Gen. 28:16–17).

Jesus Christ himself is specially localized even though he is omnipresent. Before his incarnation, he localized himself and appeared to men, sometimes as the Angel of the Lord (see Gen. 16:7–13; 22:15–18; 31:11–13; 48:15–16; Ex. 3:1–6; 14:19; Judg. 6:11–23; 13:19–20). He also appeared as a man to Joshua (Josh. 5:13–15 NASB; "Remove your sandals from your feet, for the place where you are standing is holy").

Christ was localized in a body while he was on earth and is still localized in a glorified resurrection body in heaven. Now the God-man is seated "at the right hand of the throne of the Majesty in heaven" (Heb. 8:1; see Heb. 1:3; 12:2; Col. 3:1).

At his second coming, Christ will appear to all as the glorified God-man: "Look, he is coming with the clouds, and every eye will see him" (Rev. 1:7).[6] He will be in one place at one time. Zechariah, for instance, says that "on that day his feet will stand on the Mount of Olives" (14:4).

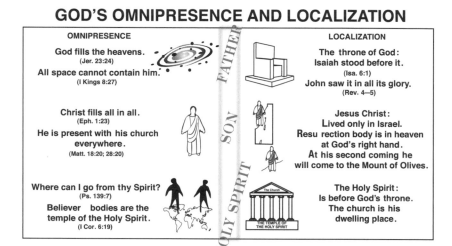

GOD'S OMNIPRESENCE AND LOCALIZATION

OMNIPRESENCE	LOCALIZATION
God fills the heavens. (Jer. 23:24) **All space cannot contain him.** (I Kings 8:27)	**The throne of God:** **Isaiah stood before it.** (Isa. 6:1) **John saw it in all its glory.** (Rev. 4—5)
Christ fills all in all. (Eph. 1:23) **He is present with his church everywhere.** (Matt. 18:20; 28:20)	**Jesus Christ:** **Lived only in Israel.** **Resu rection body is in heaven at God's right hand.** **At his second coming he will come to the Mount of Olives.**
Where can I go from thy Spirit? (Ps. 139:7) **Believer bodies are the temple of the Holy Spirit.** (I Cor. 6:19)	**The Holy Spirit:** **Is before God's throne.** **The church is his dwelling place.**

FATHER

SON

HOLY SPIRIT

The Holy Spirit, like the Father and the Son, is at once omnipresent and localized. He is in heaven before the throne of God the Father. "Grace and peace to you from him who is, and who was, and who is to come, and from the seven spirits before his throne" (Rev. 1:4). "Before the throne, seven lamps were blazing. These are the seven spirits of God" (Rev. 4:5; see 3:1; 5:6; Isa. 11:2). The Holy Spirit is also localized in the sense that he dwells in the church, the body of Christ (Eph. 2:22).

SELECTIVE INDWELLING

Even though God fills the heavens and the earth, he doesn't indwell all things. God indwells believers, but he does *not* indwell unredeemed people. This is a spiritual selectivity.

God the Father indwells those who have trusted Christ: "Jesus replied, 'If anyone loves me, he will obey my teaching. My Father will love him, and we will come to him and make our home with him'" (John 14:23). Paul also states that the Father indwells every member of the body of Christ: "one God and Father of all, who is over all and through all and in all" (Eph. 4:6).

God the Son also indwells Christians. "On that day you will realize that I am in my Father, and you are in me, and I am in you" (John 14:20; compare 14:23; 17:23, 26). Paul proclaims, "I have been crucified with Christ and I no longer live, but Christ lives in me" (Gal. 2:20). Paul also speaks about "Christ in you, the hope of glory" (Col. 1:27; see Rev. 3:20).

God the Holy Spirit indwells all believers. "However, you are not in the flesh but in the Spirit, if indeed the Spirit of God dwells in you. But if anyone does not have the Spirit of Christ, he does not belong to Him" (Rom. 8:9 NASB). "Do you not know that your body is a temple of the Holy Spirit, who is in you, whom you have received from God? You are not your own" (1 Cor. 6:19; compare John 14:17; Eph. 2:22).

The members of the Trinity indwell Christians in a similar way to how they indwell one another. Because of this, all believers will eventually have the same kind of perfect unity that exists within the Godhead (John 17:20–23; see 14:10, 20).

To summarize, God is omnipresent so that he is wholly present in all places. Yet he is also localized in special ways. He indwells some people but not all. He is somehow able to manifest his presence in different ways and in different degrees. God's heavenly throne is his ultimate dwelling place and the center of his universal dominion.

THE TRIUNE GOD INDWELLS BELIEVERS

The believer indwelt by God . . .

• the Father (Eph. 4:6)

• the Son (Gal. 2:20)

• the Holy Spirit (Rom. 8:9)

The triune God (triangle) indwells believers (circle) through the presence of Father, Son, and Holy Spirit.

Some Applications

The knowledge that God is everywhere present and that he also manifests his presence in localized ways can either be encouraging or frightening. God's special presence in the garden of Eden, once a cause of fellowship and bliss, became a source of fear to Adam and Eve after they fell into sin. Because of their sin, "they hid from the LORD God among the trees of the garden" (Gen. 3:8).

Jonah's rebellion against God led him to attempt to hide from God's presence (Jonah 1:3). But all such attempts are futile. David realized that God knows us through and through and that there is no way to escape from God's complete presence (Ps. 139:7–10).

The awareness of God's presence can truly benefit a Christian. Knowing that God is present can help a believer overcome the temptation to sin. It can also be a source of comfort and assurance, especially in times of stress, anxiety, and affliction. Even believers who have been long imprisoned for the cause of Christ in some countries are able to find consolation in the awareness of God's presence. Christ is always immediately accessible. (See Ps. 73:21–24, 28.)

One problem that hampers the lives of many Christians today is that God's omnipresence and manifest presence are only concepts to them. These truths have a place in their reasoning, but not their experience. Many of us are like Jacob, who said, "Surely the LORD is in this place, and I was not aware of it" (Gen. 28:16). We need to *practice the presence of God* in such a way that we live each day conscious that God is always with us. The person who knows Christ can *never* be alone. Our task is to become more spiritually perceptive of God's presence and increasingly aware of his nearness.

One way we can do this is through *prayer*. Ask God to make you more sensitive to his presence. Begin to prayerfully regard him as One who is constantly with you. Also, study Psalm 139 to learn how David understood and acted on these truths.

Outline of Psalm 139 "Psalm of the Attributes of God"
1. The Omniscience of God in Relation to Me (vv. 1–6)
2. The Omnipresence of God in Relation to Me (vv. 7–12)
3. The Omnipotence of God in Relation to Me (vv. 13–16)
4. The Holiness of God in Relation to Me (vv. 17–24)

A study outline of Psalm 139, with particular emphasis on personal application of the attributes of God.

Does the LORD delight in burnt offerings and sacrifices
as much as in obeying the voice of the LORD?
To obey is better than sacrifice,
and to heed is better than the fat of rams. (1 Sam. 15:22)

The sacrifices of God are a broken spirit;
a broken and a contrite heart,
O God, you will not despise. (Ps. 51:17)

Search me, O God, and know my heart;
test me and know my anxious thoughts.
See if there is any offensive way in me,
and lead me in the way everlasting. (Ps. 139:23–24)

No temptation has seized you except what is common to man. And God is faithful; he will not let you be tempted beyond what you can bear. But when you are tempted, he will also provide a way out so that you can stand up under it. (1 Cor. 10:13)

Thirty Years Later

- If I were to have written this chapter today, the material it contains would remain largely the same, since it's focused on the theological implications of timeless biblical principles.
- The chapter speaks throughout of God's omnipresence, but it is helpful to consider the specifics of the Holy Spirit's omnipresence in believers' lives. We must come to treasure and attune ourselves to his manifest presence. Facet 9 of my book *Conformed to His Image* presents the various ministries of the person of the Holy Spirit.

Chapter 10

THE TRANSCENDENT-
IMMANENT GOD

The Bible reveals God is both transcendent and immanent. His transcendence means that in his being, God is exalted above and distinct from the universe.

God's immanence means he pervades and sustains the universe. (Be sure to distinguish *immanent* from *imminent*. When something is imminent, it's impending or ready to take place.)

When we put these two concepts together, we find that God is at once both near and far. He indwells believers but is separate from them. He pervades the universe, yet he is above it and independent of it.

THE TRANSCENDENCE OF GOD

God is exalted so far above the created universe that we can't even imagine it. He is not only lofty and imminant, but he stands apart from his creation in a different quality of being. He is "the blessed and only Ruler, the King of kings and Lord of lords, who alone is immortal and who lives in unapproachable light, whom no one has seen *or can see*" (1 Tim. 6:15–16; compare John 1:18, "No one has ever seen God").

He alone is entirely separate from the things of creation, including time and space. Man and the universe aren't at all necessary to God's being or perfection. The Lord is enthroned on high and exalted above the heavens (Ps. 113:4–6; 108:5; 123:1), and "his kingdom rules over all" (Ps. 103:19).

God is the source of the immense power of the universe. There is no law or power or fate that transcends him, since he alone is the absolute Sovereign.

There's a limitless gulf between God and every creature. He is as high above a man as he is above an amoeba and as high above an archangel as he is above a man. Because God is infinite, finite differences like these are negligible to him.

But if all this is so, how can we have any positive concepts about God at all? Can we hope to think the unthinkable and comprehend the incomprehensible? Or is God so transcendent that we can say nothing meaningful about him?

The answer lies in intelligible, divine self-revelation. God is transcendent, but this doesn't mean he's in all respects unintelligible or unable to communicate with people. God has clearly revealed to us true things about his character and purposes.

As we saw in chapters 7 and 8, there is a sense in which everything, if pressed far enough, can become a mystery that goes beyond mortal man's understanding. But even though we can't see far, we *can see something*.

This is especially true in the case of God's written self-disclosure to man, the Bible. Many things in the Bible transcend human understanding, and this book has been dealing with some of them. Nevertheless, in the Bible God clearly communicates his attributes, his love for man, his plan of redemption, and so forth. In it, he reveals he is at once transcendent and immanent.

THE IMMANENCE OF GOD

Even though God is beyond this space-time universe, he is also immanent within it. He didn't simply create the universe, then withdraw to observe what would happen. Rather, the universe is a created entity that's totally dependent upon God for its continued existence.

God not only created the world; he also conserves and sustains it. He is the one who gives order and meaning to the cosmos (Col 1:17; Heb. 1:3). The universe isn't an illusion or a product of time and chance. It is real. Man can detect and study its order and design through scientific disciplines.

This concept of immanence, furthermore, relates to God's omnipresence, because the whole of God is present in every place (see chapter 9). But immanence takes us beyond the spatial idea. It focuses on God's intimacy with his creation and his personal relationship with creatures created in his image.

Christ's Sermon on the Mount emphasizes our heavenly Father's immanence. God provides food for the birds of the air and beautifully arrays the lilies of the field (Matt. 6:26–30). He counts the stars, makes the grass grow, and gives food to the beasts (Ps. 147:4–9; see Isa. 40:26). In the same way that God numbers the immense stars, he also numbers the hairs on every person's head (Matt. 10:30).

Paul spoke clearly to the Athenians about God's immanence (Acts 17:24–28). Paul said God "is not far from each one of us. 'For in him we live and move and have our being'" (vv. 27–28). Immanence is also seen in God's intimate dealings with all men. "If the LORD delights in a man's way, he makes his steps firm; though he stumble, he will not fall, for the LORD upholds him with his hand" (Ps. 37:23–24).

The fact that "a man's ways are in full view of the LORD, and he examines all his paths" (Prov. 5:21) can be comforting or disquieting depending on one's relation to God. He "knows the secrets of the heart," and no one can do anything without God's complete knowledge (Ps. 44:21; see Isa. 29:15–16; Jer. 23:23–24). But those who are rightly related to God find peace and comfort in his presence. Nothing at all can separate Christians from God's love (Rom. 8:38–39). "The eyes of the LORD are on the righteous and his ears are attentive to their cry.… The LORD is close to the brokenhearted and saves those who are crushed in spirit" (Ps. 34:15, 18).

The incarnation of the Son of God is a special example of God's immanence. The great Creator entered into our little world in a unique way. He emptied himself of his glory (Phil. 2:6–8) and submitted himself to the conditions of humanity. Even before his incarnation, Christ was immanent, but not in the same way he was afterward. The incarnation shows us what otherwise would have been hidden. "The Word became flesh and made his dwelling among us. We have seen his glory.… No one has ever seen God, but God the One and Only, who is at the Father's side, has made him known" (John 1:14, 18).

That the Father, Son, and the Holy Spirit indwell Christians is an example of God's specialized localization (see chapter 9) and also a special example of God's immanence. He is uniquely intimate with believers. However, even this is beyond our ability to imagine. What does *indwelling* mean? What mystery there is in the simple expression "you are in me, and I am in you" (John 14:20)! *Where* is God inside a Christian?

SUMMARY

God dwells in the universe, but he is nevertheless separated from it by an unbridgeable gap. God is immanent within his works but also transcendent above them. He is both near and far, intimate yet separate. "I live in a high and holy place, but also with him who is contrite and lowly in spirit" (Isa. 57:15).

Berkhof puts its this way: God is incomprehensible but yet knowable.[1] He is incomprehensible because of his transcendence but knowable because of his immanence. He is the infinite-personal God, the separate-indwelling God, the Creator-Redeemer, and the Author-Sustainer.

The transcendent-immanent God is the only adequate object of faith. Only the One who created all things (the transcendent God) has power sufficient to redeem and recreate all things (the immanent God). The creative work and the redemptive work of God are thus bound together in the Scriptures.

Many biblical passages portray God as both transcendent and immanent. Some describe God's personal appearances to different men. These include God's appearance to Moses in the burning bush on Mount Horeb (Ex. 3), his appearance to Job (Job 38:1—42:8), Isaiah's vision of God on his throne (Isa. 6), Ezekiel's vision of God's glory (Ezek. 1), and Saul's encounter with the resurrected Christ (Acts 9).

In every case, these manifestations of God produced an overwhelming sense of terror and dismay due to the transcendent God's awesome power. Each man was painfully conscious of his own sinfulness when confronted with God's glory and holiness. About such encounters with the transcendent-immanent God, Stott says:

> If the curtain that veils the unspeakable majesty of God could be drawn aside but for a moment, we too should not be able to bear the sight. As it is, we only dimly perceive how pure and brilliant must be the glory of almighty God. However, we know enough to realize that sinful man while still in his sins can never approach this holy God. A great chasm yawns between God in his righteousness and man in his sin.[2]

One of the clearest examples of the biblical balance between these two truths is in Revelation 1:9–20. The apostle John enjoyed a more intimate relationship with the Lord Jesus while he was on earth than any other man (see John 13:23; 19:26; 20:2; 21:7, 20). After Christ's ascension, this relationship continued because Christ indwelt John as he did other Christians. Nevertheless, when John saw Jesus in his glory, he "fell at his feet as though dead" (Rev. 1:17). The Lord indwells believers (immanence) but is also separate from them (transcendence).

Exodus 33:18–23, where Moses talks with God and asks to see his glory, also shows these two aspects. No man can see the face of God and live (v. 20, transcendence), but Moses was allowed to see God's "back" (v. 23, immanence). So God allowed Moses to see his glory but had to protect him from it at the same time.

TRANSCENDENCE GOD AS …	IMMANENCE GOD AS …
Infinite	Personal
Creator	Redeemer
Far	Near
Incomprehensible	Knowable
Separate	Indwelling
Independent of the Universe	Pervading the Universe
Author of the Creation	Sustainer of the Creation
Apart	Intimate
Burning Holiness	Self-sacrificing Love
Almighty	Friend

A summary of the comparisons of transcendence and immanence

THE EXTREMES

Two natural extremes relate to the transcendence-immanence mystery. The transcendence extreme minimizes or denies God's immanence. Modern examples are found in Deism, some groups within Judaism; and Barth and Brunner, who tend to view God as "wholly Other."[3]

Deists emphasize human reason rather than revelation. The universe doesn't depend on God. They view God as wholly transcendent and so out of reach that he might just as well not exist.

The immanence extreme minimizes or denies God's transcendence. The more popular current examples are pantheism, panentheism, naturalism and humanism, and the "social gospel."

Pantheism (monism) sees God as the process of history; he is the soul and reason of the universe. God is in us and we are all God.

Panentheism (process theology) is a liberal approach to natural theology that attacks the supernatural, transcendent idea of God.[4] Process theologians have abandoned the supernatural God. Thus they are left with evolution instead of creation, "relationship" instead of redemption, and "analogy in human experience" instead of revelation.

Naturalists and humanists have an antitranscendent outlook, allowing only the immanent. They hope history somehow contains its own meaning. Given enough time, man will understand the world and all significant truth without having to turn to a reference point outside of himself. This is a man-centered faith in human potential.

The social gospel strips all transcendent elements from Christianity and humanizes all religion, including the concept of God. God is reduced to such a level that men shouldn't submit to him; they should just cooperate with him. Religion's only purpose is to serve man, not God.[5]

We see from these brief examples that serious error is introduced when anyone minimizes or denies either of these biblical truths. The transcendence extreme leads to the idea of a God who is so "wholly Other" that he can't be personally known or communicated with. The immanence extreme reduces God to our level and effectively destroys all hope for the redemption of sinful men and a fallen universe.

The only way to represent the biblical picture of reality is to acknowledge the revealed fact that God is *both* transcendent *and* immanent. The two truths must be kept in dynamic tension, knowing that from God's higher perspective, they're friends, not enemies. Only the transcendent-immanent God can be at once the infinite Creator and the personal Redeemer.

SOME APPLICATIONS

One way to apply the biblical doctrine of the transcendent-immanent God to daily living is to connect it with the idea of "the fear of the Lord." Because the almighty God is immanent, he genuinely affects every part of our lives. His greatness and his transcendence require our utmost regard, respect, and esteem.

The biblical concept of fear is that, like faith, it can be good or bad depending on the object in which it's placed. "Fear of man will prove to be a snare, but whoever trusts in the LORD is kept safe" (Prov. 29:25). The problem is that unless God is one's ultimate "fear-object,"[6] the things man reveres and fears losing don't properly reflect reality. Instead of bowing to reality, they distort it by fearing other things more than the living God. Many people, for example, fear the loss of worldly status more than they fear a wrong relationship with God.

No one or nothing should be revered as much as God. Unfortunately, most people repress their thoughts about God, resist him, or rationalize him away. They revere such things as success, financial security, and friendships much more than God. This can happen with Christians who lean too much in the immanence direction and forget God's transcendence. Even in Christian circles, there's a temptation to revere other things more than God (for instance, the desire to be accepted and esteemed by a group or organization).

When people forget or ignore God's transcendence, God becomes so immanent that he's no longer a fear-object, and this leads to sin: "When men no longer fear God, they transgress his laws without hesitation."[7] (See Ps. 36:1; Eccl. 8:11.)

Believers should maintain the concept of God as awesome and dreadful, remembering at the same time that he is also immanent. This does not mean that the believer in Christ should be afraid of God as a person, for the real Christian knows that God loves him and gave his Son for him. But we should never forget who God is.

When Christians minimize either God's immanence or transcendence, they tend to forget his awesomeness and holiness. Their attitudes and actions may reflect a self-assurance and disrespect for God. Some believers speak of God in a flippant manner, using glib phrases like "jamming with Jesus" as though the "high and lofty One" (Isa. 57:15) were a rock star.

Another area requiring a balanced view of the transcendent-immanent God is the nature of God's indwelling. The triune God dwells in every Christian. But there's sometimes so much emphasis placed on the fact that Christ indwells believers that we fail to remember that Christ as the God-man is in heaven at the Father's right hand.

TRANSCENDENCE-IMMANENCE BIBLICAL PERSONAGES	EMPHASIS
Job (Job 38:1; 42:2)	• Revelation of God's power and wisdom • Job's confession, submission, and worship
Moses (Ex. 3)	• God in the burning bush • Moses' worship, submission, and commission
Elijah (1 Kings 19)	• God's power and still small voice • Elijah's submission and recommission
Isaiah (Isa. 6) and Ezekiel (Ezek. 1)	• God's throne and glory • Their worship, submission, and commission
Saul/Paul (Acts 9)	• The glory of the resurrected Christ • Paul's subjection and commission
John (Rev. 1)	• Appearance of the glorified Christ • John's worship and commission

"THE FEAR OF THE LORD"
DEFINITION: PROFOUND REVERENCE FOR THE MAJESTY AND HOLINESS OF GOD RESULTING IN PROPER WORSHIP AND SERVICE
1. It is the beginning of knowledge (Prov. 1:7)
2. It is the beginning of wisdom (Ps. 111:10; Prov. 9:10)
3. It is clean—totally pure (Ps. 19:9)
4. It can be taught (Ps. 34:11)
5. It is to hate evil (Prov. 8:13)
6. It prolongs life (Prov. 10:27)
7. It is dependable (Prov. 14:26)
8. It is meaningful (Prov. 14:27)
9. It should be continuous (Prov. 23:17)
10. It is a testimony to others (Job 1:8)
11. (Others—see a concordance)

Though Christ is in believers, the New Testament speaks much more about believers being "in Christ." A proper emphasis on who we are and what we have in him (see Eph. 1—3) will avoid an overbalance into internal mysticism. We should focus on the work going on in heaven at God's right hand on our behalf, where Christ is interceding for us (Rom. 8:34).

The transcendence-immanence mystery relates to other mysteries and to different facets of the Christian life. In the problem of evil, for example (chapter 5), God in his holiness is outraged at sin (transcendence), but he continues to sustain the world and personally suffers because of the sin (immanence). God doesn't watch the world with detached interest; he is involved.

In prayer and worship, believers can sense both the otherness and the nearness of God. Though God is enthroned in his transcendence, he is at the same time very near in his graciousness and immanence.

When we see the Lord Jesus Christ face-to-face, what we now dimly perceive about the transcendent-immanent God will become much more clear. Perhaps we'll react as did two of the animals in *The Wind in the Willows* when they saw "the Piper at the Gate of Dawn":

> "Rat!" he found breath to whisper, shaking. "Are you afraid?"
>
> "Afraid?" murmured the Rat, his eyes shining with unutterable love. "Afraid! Of *him*? O, never, never! And yet—and yet—O Mole, I am afraid!"
>
> Then the two animals, crouching to the earth, bowed their heads and did worship.[8]

> The fear of the LORD is the beginning of wisdom, and knowledge of the Holy One is understanding. (Prov. 9:10)

> And now, O Israel, what does the LORD your God ask of you but to fear the LORD your God, to walk in all his ways, to love him, to serve the LORD your God with all your heart and with all your soul. (Deut. 10:12)

> But for you who revere my name, the sun of righteousness will rise with healing in its wings. And you will go out and leap like calves released from the stall. (Mal. 4:2)

> Great and marvelous are your deeds,
> Lord God Almighty.
> Just and true are your ways,
> King of the ages.
> Who will not fear you, O Lord,
> and bring glory to your name?
> For you alone are holy.

All nations will come
and worship before you,
for your righteous acts have been revealed. (Rev. 15:3–4)

Come, let us sing for joy to the LORD;
let us shout aloud to the Rock of our salvation.
Let us come before him with thanksgiving
and extol him with music and song.
For the LORD is the great God,
the great King above all gods....
Come, let us bow down in worship,
let us kneel before the LORD our Maker;
for he is our God
and we are the people of his pasture,
the flock under his care. (Ps. 95:1–3, 6–7)

To him who is able to keep you from falling and to present you
before his glorious presence without fault and with great joy—to the
only God our Savior be glory, majesty, power and authority, through
Jesus Christ our Lord, before all ages, now and forevermore! (Jude
vv. 24–25)

THIRTY YEARS LATER

- The original text focuses on God's relationship with his creation through his being and action. It would also be good to add a word on the active role believers are privileged to play in God's immanence through prayer, service to others, and the gifts of the Spirit. Without God's grace immanent in the world, we cannot fulfill the things he gives us to accomplish in synergistic participation with him. As Augustine put it, "Without God we cannot, and without us he will not." The spiritual life always requires our action and consent to God's multifaceted and life-affirming call.
- George Herbert's poem "The Elixir" dramatically exemplifies the truth God imparts to us which enables us to see his immanence in the world and in our lives.

Teach me, my God and King,
In all things thee to see,
And what I do in anything,
To do it as for thee:

Not rudely, as a beast,
To run into an action;
But still to make thee prepossessed,
And give it his perfection.

A man that looks on glass,
On it may stay his eye;
Or if he pleaseth, through it pass,
And then heav'n espy.

All may of thee partake:
Nothing can be so mean,
Which with his tincture (for thy sake)
Will not grow bright and clean.

A servant with this clause
Makes drudgery divine:
Who sweeps a room, as for thy laws,
Makes that and th' action fine.

This is the famous stone
That turneth all to gold:
For that which God doth touch and own
Cannot for less be told.

- God transcends space and time; these are part of his created order. Our consciousness, however, is bound to space and time. Hence, the error in the question, "Where did God come from?"
- The history of spiritual formation distinguishes two approaches to the knowledge of God, though there is really a spectrum with the two on opposite poles. This spectrum can range from a purely *kataphatic* orientation to a purely *apophatic* orientation. *Kataphatic* is from a Greek word meaning "affirmative," and this tradition, more characteristic of the Western church, stresses

knowing God through general and special revelation. The term *apophatic* is derived from a Greek word that means "negative," and this tradition, more characteristic of the Eastern church, stresses God's transcendence and mystery. Thus, a *kataphatic* style of spirituality uses symbols, images, and metaphors while an *apophatic* style emphasizes God's hiddenness. This chapter affirms them as both-and rather than either-or.

- Another description of "the fear of the Lord" is the recognition of something greater than us that we consider impossible to control. Control is a central issue in the spiritual life, since it is the human heart's natural disposition to pursue the arrogance of autonomy rather than the humility of radical dependence. The illusion of control is a seductive dream.

Chapter 11

POSITIONAL VERSUS EXPERIENTIAL TRUTH

G od views us in Christ as perfect. Nevertheless, we are still prone to sin. The implications of these two contrary descriptions of saved people are so profound they are unsearchable.

THE BELIEVER'S POSITION IN CHRIST

The mystery of the work of the cross is beyond comprehension. When someone appropriates the work of the cross by trusting in Christ, he is instantly placed in union with Christ. This union is so real that the believer has actually died and risen with Christ. The believer is included in the whole process of Christ's death, burial, resurrection, and present life in such a way that these things become completely identified with him. The Christian's life is now bound up with the life Christ lives before the Father.

God cannot lower his standards; he doesn't grade on a curve. God's standard of righteousness is complete perfection. Christ said, "Be perfect, therefore, as your heavenly Father is perfect" (Matt. 5:48). Jesus Christ's substitutionary work was the only possible way in which God could justify (declare righteous) sinful men without compromising his own holiness (Rom. 3:26).

The Bible presents an astonishing array of privileges that belong to a person the moment he becomes a child of God through faith in Jesus. Many of these blessings are discussed by Paul in the first three chapters of Ephesians. Others are found throughout the New Testament. Some of the better-known ones are mentioned below; a more complete list with Scripture has been complied most ably by Lewis Sperry Chafer.[1]

Each of these positional truths, mind you, is the present possession of *every* believer (I am using the term "positional truth" to mean what is *actually* true of a believer here and now by virtue of his or her identification with Christ).

Believers are all in God's eternal plan (see chapter 4). All Christians have been *redeemed* (purchased out of bondage to sin; Gal. 5:1; Eph. 1:7) and *reconciled* to God (2 Cor. 5:20–21). God has *forgiven* all the believer's trespasses (Eph. 1:7; Col. 2:13) and has *adopted* him into God's family (Gal. 4:4–7; Eph. 1:4–5).

In his letter to the Romans, Paul concentrates on the fact that God has declared Christians righteous (*justified*; Rom. 3:24, 26; 4:5; 5:1). Peter writes that believers in Christ are "a chosen people, a royal priesthood, a holy nation, a people belonging to God" (1 Peter 2:9).

Each person in Christ has direct access to God and his grace (Rom. 5:1–2; Eph. 2:18; Heb. 4:16). God is devoted to believers and cares for them in many striking ways (Rom. 5:8–10).

God tells us that Christians are already as good as *glorified* (Rom. 8:30), for God sees believers as they will be: perfect and complete in Christ (Col. 2:9–10). We've already been given "every spiritual blessing in Christ" (Eph. 1:3).

These positional blessings can't be earned, since they are not related to human merit. Neither are they progressive in character, for they're all given to the believer at the moment of salvation. They don't depend on how we feel, for they're not emotionally experienced by the believer (Christians don't "feel" justification or sanctification).

The believer's position in Christ is eternal, because God gives these things to us as gifts we don't deserve. They're based on God's grace, not human effort; and consequently, God will not revoke them. God alone makes these things possible, not man. If it weren't for his revelation to man, we wouldn't even know they were available to us as a free gift.

UNION WITH CHRIST
Blessed in the heavenly realms with every spiritual blessing (1:3)
Recipients of God's grace (1:6)
Redeemed (1:7)
Chosen, having been predestined (1:11)
Sealed by the Holy Spirit (1:13)
Created to do good works (2:10)
Brought near to God (2:13)
Built up as the church of Jesus Christ (2:21–22)
Indwelt by the Holy Spirit (2:22)
Sharers of God's promise (3:6)
Freedom and confidence in approaching God (3:12)

Facets of the believer's union with Christ (see Eph. 1—3, especially the expression, "in Christ").

THE BELIEVER'S DAILY EXPERIENCE

In spite of all these wonderful positional truths, Christians still sin in thought, word, and deed. Although we've been cleansed from sin and made perfect in God's sight because of Christ's righteousness, our daily experiences are imperfect.

From the believer's own perspective, he is painfully aware of his sinfulness (that is, if he is being honest with himself). None of us can attain a state of sinless perfection in this life. We can't reach a plateau of complete purity as long as the law of sin is in our members (Rom. 7:14–25). John made this abundantly clear in 1 John 1:5—2:2. "If we claim to be without sin, we deceive ourselves and the truth is not in us" (1:8). John says here that every believer still has the problem of sin. We'd only be deceiving ourselves if we denied this truth.

John also refers to specific manifestations of the flesh: "If we claim we have not sinned, we make him out to be a liar" (1:10). There's no question that believers commit sins. John says that it would compound the problem for a believer to act as though he didn't sin when he did. Instead, we should confess our sins for what they really are before the Lord, knowing that Christ is our advocate with the Father (1:9; 2:1–2).

The flesh is still in the Christian even though he has also received a new nature, "created to be like God in true righteousness and holiness" (Eph. 4:24). Now the Christian has choices he didn't have before he received Christ. By the exercise of his will he can choose to walk in the Spirit or walk in the flesh (Rom. 8:3–9; Gal. 5:15–26).

However, no matter how passionately a believer may desire a life that conforms perfectly to his position in the heavenlies, he can't always maintain this standard. The most pious and godly men and women through the centuries have acknowledged their utter corruption before the Holy God. As we grow in Christ, we also become more conscious of our own sinfulness, and thus more appreciative of God's grace. The apostle Paul described his life as a constant struggle of the old against the new (Rom. 7:14—8:2). He wrote, "I do not understand what I do. For what I want to do I do not do, but what I hate I do.... For what I do is not the good I want to do; no, the evil I do not want to do—this I keep on doing" (vv. 15, 19). Paul undoubtedly found a much more victorious life than this (see 7:24—25), but he was also able to distinguish the reality of a defeated Christian life from his position in the heavenlies in Christ Jesus. This is why he could victoriously proclaim, "Therefore, there is now no condemnation for those who are in Christ Jesus" (8:1).

Clearly there is a great difference between our subjective experience of salvation and our objective salvation that's secure at the right hand of the Father. There's a difference between the believer's state (experiential truth) and his standing (positional truth). The believer's state is changeable, but his standing is unchangeable.[2] The real difficulty lies in understanding how both things can be true of a person at once.

How to Avoid the Extremes

The spirit and the flesh (i.e., the power of sin in our members; Rom. 7:21–23) are contrary to one another (Gal. 5:17), but believers in Christ have both. Because of the reality of both positional truth and experiential truth, the believer is at once a saint and a sinner. God will not indwell an unclean vessel, but he indwells every Christian. Even though he knows we still sin, he also sees the righteousness of Christ Jesus placed on our account. In addition, he sees us as we will be, when our sin will be removed (this relates to the mystery of time we addressed earlier).

Two basic extremes can arise if Christians don't properly approach positional and experiential truth.

The first extreme results from minimizing positional truth. This produces a mentality of fear and insecurity. Unaware of his position in Christ, the believer doesn't understand that God fully recognizes how bad he is yet accepts him through the merits of Christ.

Such a person is still operating on a performance basis, hoping to please God, but constantly afraid of being exposed. He falsely equates his experience with the status of his salvation, and he is, therefore, still under the curse of "religiosity." He may feel that unless he confesses all his sins he will not be positionally forgiven and in danger of losing his salvation.

Even if salvation were based 99 percent on Christ's work and 1 percent on human effort, there could be no genuine security and peace with God. Everyone would be worrying about that 1 percent. The only foundation on which a real love relationship with God can be built is the biblical revelation that Christ has paid for all the believer's sins.

Only God himself could satisfy his demand for complete righteousness. This is why it's so important for believers to *reckon by faith* that the positional things God says about them are really so.

The second extreme results from minimizing our experiential walk. Some believers feel that since they're rightly related to God positionally, they can be careless about being right experientially.

The Bible says, "*If we confess* our sins, he is faithful and just and will forgive us our sins and purify us from all unrighteousness" (1 John 1:9). Some shrug that *if* phrase off with, "My sins have already been forgiven!" But John isn't denying that Christ has positionally forgiven the believer's sins. Rather, he is writing about the believer's fellowship with a holy God. While sin and disobedience cannot annul a Christian's position, they can and will seriously mar his walk with God.

It's important to notice that the believer's position versus his experience ties in closely with the divine sovereignty/human responsibility mystery (chapter 4). Divine sovereignty connects with the believer's position, and human responsibility relates to his experience. Therefore, the same balance that's required in our approach to divine sovereignty and human responsibility is also essential to a proper understanding of positional and experiential truth.

Even though our position is secure with God, we shouldn't adopt the attitude that we can do as we please. We're still responsible to live a life of quality that reflects our heavenly position to the world. In one way, we should be sure to distinguish position and experience, especially in the area of salvation. But in another way, position and experience should be joined together.

The believer's position ought to be the basis for his experience. This is clearly seen in an epistle like Ephesians. After Paul outlines the believer's position in the heavenlies (Eph. 1—3), he then builds a whole series of imperatives (Eph. 4—6) on this foundation. There are no commands in the positional section of the book because these are things that have been accomplished by God alone. But then the imperatives begin to appear, always based on positional truth.

WHEN EXPERIENCE WILL EQUAL POSITION

There's a constant struggle in Christians between the mortal remnant of the old man in Adam and the new man in Christ, and *nothing* can eliminate it until the "sin that so easily entangles" (Heb. 12:1) is fully removed. Only then will the believer's experience perfectly conform to his position. Until that time, we must trust God to bring our experience closer to our position.

When will perfection come? Paul says that we're groaning inwardly as we eagerly await the redemption of our bodies (Rom. 8:23). He also says that believers "must all appear before the judgment seat of Christ" (2 Cor. 5:10) and that each man's "work will be shown for what it is" on that day (1 Cor. 3:13). This is a resurrection of life and a judgment of rewards for those who "hear the voice of the Son of God" and "those who have done good will rise to live, and those who have done evil will rise to be condemned" (John 5:25, 29). Even if all of a believer's work is burned up, "he will suffer loss; he himself will be saved, but only as one escaping through the flames" (1 Cor. 3:15).

At the judgment seat of Christ, the flesh—our propensity to sin—will be stripped from us. As our dead works are being burned up, it may possibly be the first time that we see our sins as Christ sees them. From then on, our experience will be identical with our position because the capacity to sin will be gone. "Thanks be to God—through Jesus Christ our Lord" (Rom. 7:25)!

APPLICATIONS

Believers must clearly focus on two things: the divine side of salvation (position) and human responsibility (experience). When positional truth is properly understood, it can become a great aid to our daily experience. This is why Paul said that we're to consciously consider our position in Christ to be true, regardless of how we feel.

> In the same way, count yourselves dead to sin but alive to God in Christ Jesus. Therefore do not let sin reign in your mortal body so that you obey its evil desires. Do not offer the parts of your body to sin, as instruments of wickedness, but rather offer yourselves to God, as those who have been brought from death to life; and offer the parts of your body to him as instruments of righteousness. (Rom. 6:11–13)

Not only are we to reckon our position as true in our lives; we must also *act* (human responsibility) on the basis of this truth. Even though we possess every spiritual blessing (Eph. 1:3), these will do nothing for our everyday life unless we start to use them. Too many Christians live like spiritual paupers because they ignore the limitless riches God makes available to them.

Therefore, since we have been justified through faith, we have peace with God through our Lord Jesus Christ, through whom we have gained access by faith into this grace in which we now stand. And we rejoice in the hope of the glory of God. (Rom. 5:1–2)

Therefore, if anyone is in Christ, he is a new creation; the old has gone, the new has come (2 Cor. 5:17).

I have been crucified with Christ and I no longer live, but Christ lives in me. The life I live in the body, I live by faith in the Son of God, who loved me and gave himself for me. (Gal. 2:20)

For you did not receive a spirit that makes you a slave again to fear, but you received the Spirit of sonship. And by him we cry, "*Abba*, Father." (Rom. 8:15)

Since, then, you have been raised with Christ, set your hearts on things above, where Christ is seated at the right hand of God. Set your minds on things above, not on earthly things. For you died, and your life is now hidden with Christ in God. When Christ, who is your life, appears, then you also will appear with him in glory. (Col. 3:1–4)

For he has rescued us from the dominion of darkness and brought us into the kingdom of the Son he loves, in whom we have redemption, the forgiveness of sins. (Col. 1:13–14)

And this is my prayer: that your love may abound more and more in knowledge and depth of insight, so that you may be able to discern what is best and may be pure and blameless until the day of Christ, filled with the fruit of righteousness that comes through Jesus Christ—to the glory and praise of God. (Phil. 1:9–11)

THIRTY YEARS LATER

- This chapter could well have been titled "Experiential and Positional Grace," since it stresses the grace of salvation and sanctification. In the Christian life, there's no choice between them, but an embrace of both.
- There is a distinction between the actual truth of our identification with Christ and our actual experience of this transforming reality.

THE BELIEVER'S STATE	THE BELIEVER'S STANDING
position	condition
credited to us	experienced by us
saint	sinner
unchangeable	changeable
legal, judicial	moral

- Three evidences point beyond themselves to God's reality: (1) the world around us (the "'problem' of good" and the "glory of creation"); (2) our inherent, inner feelings of right and wrong, just and unjust, duty and obligation; and (3) the revealing of God's power through Christlike attributes and actions in our relationships with others and their actions toward us. Each is manifest on both the experiential and positional levels.

Chapter 12

THE WORD OF GOD

I believe that God has revealed himself to men, and that revelation is the Bible." Thus we started at the book's beginning, and there we stand: The Bible is *the* authority for truth. However, even God's revealed Word involves a mysterious element beyond human comprehension. Like the God-man, the Bible is completely divine and completely human at once.

THE BIBLE IS A PRODUCT OF GOD

Revelation has been defined as God communicating to man things man wouldn't otherwise know. If this is carried back far enough, it includes a great deal, so revelation is often divided into two basic kinds: (1) natural or general revelation and (2) supernatural or special revelation. According to Scripture, the creation itself reveals things about God, including his existence, his divine nature, and his eternal power (Ps. 19:1–4; Rom. 1:18–20). This revelation is sufficient to condemn those who reject God (Rom. 1:20, "men are without excuse").

But God reveals much more about himself through special revelation. He took the initiative in revelation and did it through various means.

He revealed himself by special actions and appearances to people (the pillar of fire and the Angel of the Lord). He often spoke to people in dreams and visions. Sometimes he used special means of revelation like the Urim and Thummim on the high priest's breastplate or casting lots. More often, however, he communicated directly to people as he did with Moses, the prophets, and the apostles.

The *climax* of revelation, called personal revelation, was realized in the incarnation of Jesus Christ, the God-man (see John 1:18; 14:9; Col. 1:15; Heb. 1:1–3).

One type of special revelation is written revelation. The Bible isn't only a record of revelation; it's also a revelation itself. This is so because the very act of writing Scripture was personally superintended by God the Holy Spirit. This is part of the biblical doctrine of *inspiration*.

Ryrie defines inspiration as "God's superintendence of the human authors so that, using their own individual personalities, they composed and recorded without error his revelation to man in the words of the original autographs."[1] There's no way to understand how God worked with the human authors so that the resultant Scripture was at once *their own writings* and *God's infallible Word*. This is the mystery.

The Bible clearly claims to be a product of God. "All Scripture is God-breathed and is useful for teaching, rebuking, correcting and training in righteousness" (2 Tim. 3:16). Scripture is the breath of God.

A similar passage says: "Prophecy never had its origin in the will of man, but men spoke from God as they were carried along by the Holy Spirit" (2 Peter 1:21). Combining these verses, "inspiration is the process by which Spirit-moved writers recorded God-breathed writings."[2]

Inspiration applies to *all* parts of all canonical (inspired) books. Because the inspired Scriptures partake of God's nature, they are without error. Everything the Bible teaches is true, including its historical and factual statements. The very words themselves were inspired in the original manuscripts (see Jer. 26:2; Matt. 5:18; Luke 16:17; 24:44; John 10:35; Rom. 3:2; 15:4; 1 Cor. 2:13; Heb. 10:7; 2 Peter 3:16; Rev. 22:18–19). Christ and Paul built whole arguments on specific words used in the Old Testament (see Matt. 22:41–45; John 10:34–36; Gal. 3:16).

It's clear that the doctrine of inspiration applies to the original manuscripts, not to translations and later manuscripts. Nevertheless, the science of textual criticism (or "lower criticism") demonstrates the accuracy of our

Hebrew and Greek manuscripts. Only small details are in question, and none of these affect any biblical doctrine. Our Bibles are substantially pure, and they can be received with confidence as virtually inspired.[3]

Men have held and taught inadequate and unbiblical theories of inspiration throughout church history.

One theory proposes that inspiration is a natural (though God-given) genius for expression. It teaches that the Bible is inspired in the same way that great art is inspired.

Another theory sees men of God being given special understanding of God's will and recording their insights in the books that came to be included in the Bible. This, however, is not inspiration but illumination, a ministry of the Holy Spirit that gives us spiritual understanding of biblical truths.

The neoorthodox view states the Bible *becomes* the Word of God only in an existential experience or a crisis encounter with God.

The endorsement theory holds that God simply gave his stamp of approval to the spiritual writings of godly men. These writings become his Word because he uses them in blessing men.

The concept theory teaches that God gave the human authors his inspired ideas or concepts. These authors then expressed the concepts in their own words.

Another theory teaches that the Bible contains different degrees of inspiration. That is, the control by the Holy Spirit in inspiration fluctuates with the receptivity of the human authors and/or the character of the material. A variation of this theory is the idea that only parts of the Bible are inspired: namely, those portions of Scripture that couldn't have been written by unaided men.

The (mechanical) dictation theory regards the human writers as secretaries who simply recorded the dictation of God. Liberal theologians sometimes build this idea into a straw man that they claim represents the conservative position. When they knock it over, they assume that they've refuted the "fundamentalists." But in reality, virtually no evangelical theologians hold this view. They recognize that the human writers were involved as authors of the Scripture.

THEORIES OF INSPIRATION
1. Natural = gifted, intelligent men wrote the Bible
2. Mystical = recorded religious experiences
3. Crisis = inspired only when "felt"
4. Endorsement = God approved certain writings
5. Concept = only the concepts are inspired
6. Degrees = certain books are more inspired than others
7. Dictation = God dictated the exact words to secretaries

These are seven of the theories of inspiration. The first six usually characterize liberal and neoorthodox views. The seventh is a "straw man" caricature of the evangelical position.

It's clear that the Bible repeatedly claims to be a direct product of God. It's fully inspired in all its words and parts (verbal, plenary inspiration). It is God's propositional revelation to all people, breathed by the Spirit of God. The stamp of "thus says the Lord" pervades its pages. This is why the Bible accomplishes such phenomenal results in lives (see Isa. 55:11).

The Bible is unlike any other book; its author constantly goes with it and empowers it according to his purpose. It's a living book because it's animated by the Holy Spirit. "For the word of God is living and active. Sharper than any double-edged sword, it penetrates even to dividing soul and spirit, joints and marrow; it judges the thoughts and attitudes of the heart" (Heb. 4:12).

THE VITAL NECESSITY
OF THE WORD OF GOD
TO CHRISTIAN LIVING

2 Timothy 3:16—"All Scripture is inspired by God and profitable for ...

SCRIPTURE · *TEACHING* · **SCRIPTURE**

- as a foundation
- revealing God, Christ, and salvation
- presenting basic principles of life

answering the great philosophical questions:
1. "Who am I?" (Self-identity)
2. "Where did I come from?" (Origins)
3. "Where am I going?" (Destiny)

REPROOF

- showing how and where biblical principles have been violated
- as a mirror
- revealing conflicts in key relationships

revealing
1. rejection of self
2. wrong reactions to God
3. failure in marital relations or difficulties in dating relationships
4. conflicts within the family
5. inneffective friendships
6. tensions on the job
7. purposelessness for future

CORRECTION

- as a prescription
- presenting responsible steps of corrective action
- revealing the pattern for godly conduct

giving

What to Do	How to Do It
1.	1.
2.	2.
3.	3.
4.	4.
5.	5.

TRAINING

- as a lifetime project
- giving instruction for a continuing reinforcement of the basic steps of corrective action

building a Christian life
- Worship (Godward)
- Edification (saintward)
- Witness (worldward)
- Fellowship
- Purpose
- Transformation
- Doctrine

THE BIBLE IS A PRODUCT OF MEN

The Bible is not only completely divine, but also completely human. This isn't difficult to demonstrate, since the human authors of so many of the books are clearly identified. The authors of most of the psalms name themselves (David, Asaph, and others). Solomon says he wrote most of Proverbs, and the prophets identify their works as well. The authors of most of the New Testament books record their names in the opening sentences.

The humanity of the biblical books is also supported by the obvious personality and literary differences. The writers had differing styles, vocabularies, grammar, and backgrounds. These differences are seen in translations, and they're even more evident in the original languages. Also, the Scriptures express personal human desires and thoughts. For example, Paul wrote: "When you come, bring the cloak that I left with Carpus at Troas, and my scrolls, especially the parchments" (2 Tim. 4:13). This doesn't sound like a passage simply dictated to Paul by God. It was Paul who needed his cloak, not God!

The Uniqueness of Biblical Revelation

The biblical doctrine of revelation is unique, since it alone claims to be equally a product of God and man. The Bible is a completely divine and completely human book in a way we cannot comprehend. Other so-called scriptures either claim to be the insights of spiritual sages (the Hindu scriptures) or dictated messages from God (the Qur'an and the Book of Mormon). Only the Bible is a divine-human revelation. Its content is infinitely deep, but it's couched in finite human language.

This mystery parallels the divine sovereignty/human responsibility mystery. The Bible is God's revelation to man, and his sovereignty ensured that it is completely authoritative and inspired. But this doesn't mean God restricted the various human authors' free will. Instead, they were able to exercise their wills and human responsibilities even while writing the words that were at once both human and divine.

The Two Extremes

People don't naturally arrive at the proper view of Scripture. A mystery exists here and gives rise to two natural extremes. One minimizes the Bible's divine aspect by humanizing it; the other minimizes the Bible's human aspect by deifying it.

The first extreme states that since the Bible was written by humans, it can't also be God's pure revelation. It contains great truths, but being human in origin, it's not free from error.

The popularity of this view is seen in the prevalence of the inadequate theories of inspiration mentioned earlier. All but the last of these play down (in varying degrees) the Scriptures' divine aspect. These theories adequately explain the Bible's human aspect (personality, stylistic, vocabulary, and grammatical differences), but at the great cost of weakening or completely eliminating the divine. They fail to honor the Bible's own claims to be more than just the writings of men.

The second extreme is represented by the (mechanical) dictation theory. This view does not account for the human aspect of the Bible that is seen in the personality and literary differences. It can also lead to bibliolatry (the worship of the Bible instead of the God who revealed it).

THE ANALOGY TO THE GOD-MAN

There's a close parallel between Christ as the living Word and the Scriptures as the written Word of God. Both the Savior and the Scriptures have divine-human natures. In both cases the process by which this came about is beyond human comprehension.

In the case of the God-man, God joined with humanity to produce "the holy one to be born" (Luke 1:35). This verse teaches that the Holy Spirit came upon Mary and the power of the Most High overshadowed her. In the case of the written Word, God again joined with humanity to produce his holy Word. The Holy Spirit moved men to speak from God (2 Peter 1:21). Because of this, the living Word is sinless and the written Word is without error (in the original manuscripts).[4]

On the negative side, the analogy between the two Words can be seen in the way that both can and have been abused by the same two extremes, one minimizing the Word's divinity and the other its humanity. The only proper approach is to trust God and bow to his greater wisdom by acknowledging the complete divinity and humanity of Christ and the Scriptures.

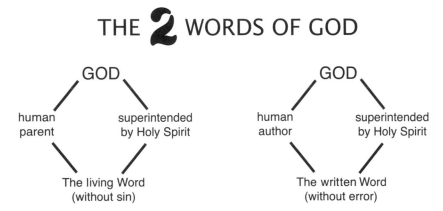

The comparison between Jesus Christ, the living Word, and the Bible, the written Word.

SOME APPLICATIONS

Just as the Bible is the result of a divine-human process, it requires a divine-human process for people to appreciate it and understand it properly. The difference is that the "encoding" of the Word was infallible, but its "decoding" is fallible.

To understand the truths of God's Word, Christians must place themselves under the Holy Spirit's guidance. Apart from this illuminating ministry of the Holy Spirit, there can be no spiritual receptiveness to God's truths. This is the divine aspect of the process. Tozer comments, "There is no truth apart from the Spirit. The most brilliant intellect may be imbecilic when confronted with the mysteries of God. For a man to understand revealed truth requires an act of God equal to the original act which inspired the text."[5]

The human aspect of the decoding process is also critical. Illumination must be accompanied by logical consistency on our part. Certain basic interpretive principles must be followed in attempting to understand the Bible. This is the science of hermeneutics.

We should approach the Scriptures in a plain and normal fashion. Each passage should be examined in the light of the immediate and broad context. If a symbol or parable or figure of speech is being used, the context will generally make this clear.

The Bible should be understood in a historical and grammatical way, and this in-context approach must be applied consistently to all parts of the Scriptures. Furthermore, Scripture is its own best interpreter. We should always allow the clear passages to interpret the unclear.

When these principles of hermeneutics aren't consistently followed, difficulties arise. Thus, various cults make the Bible say what they want it to say by simply pulling passages out of context.

Every time we read the Bible we should remember that our understanding of it must be a divine-human process. This is why it's wise to pray for the Holy Spirit's guidance and illumination before we study Scripture. Whenever we open the Bible, we should also ask God to enable us to apply what we learn from it.

Witnessing is another divine-human process. The Spirit of God works through the Word of God in the hands of the children of God to bring people to Christ. God has chosen to work through people to lead other people to the Savior. Witnessing is most effective when the Word of God is unleashed in the hands of believers.

Finally, believers need to develop a greater appreciation for the Word. God has given us an infinite revelation that has the answers for which people are searching. We should praise God for his written revelation. It gives us wisdom, instruction, correction, and encouragement (Rom. 15:4; 2 Tim. 3:16). But it also always demands a response from the reader.

1. Hearing (Rom. 10:17)
2. Reading (Rev. 1:3)
3. Singing (Col. 3:16)
4. Studying (Acts 17:11)
5. Memorizing (Ps. 119:11)
6. Meditating (Josh. 1:8)

The Star Illustration, portraying the six means of taking in the Word of God for ourselves.

You have said:

> Do not let this Book of the Law depart from your mouth; meditate
> on it day and night, so that you may be careful to do everything
> written in it. Then you will be prosperous and successful. (Josh. 1:8)

> I meditate on your precepts
> and consider your ways.
> I delight in your decrees;
> I will not neglect your word.

> Do good to your servant, and I will live;
> I will obey your word.
> Open my eyes that I may see
> wonderful things in your law. (Ps. 119:15–18)

> Your word is a lamp to my feet
> and a light for my path. (Ps. 119:105)

> For Ezra had devoted himself to the study and observance of the
> Law of the LORD, and to teaching its decrees and laws in Israel. (Ezra
> 7:10)

> All Scripture is God-breathed and is useful for teaching, rebuking,
> correcting and training in righteousness, so that the man of God
> may be thoroughly equipped for every good work. (2 Tim. 3:16–17)

> The word of God is living and active. Sharper than any double-edged
> sword, it penetrates even to dividing soul and spirit, joints and mar-
> row; it judges the thoughts and attitudes of the heart. Nothing in all
> creation is hidden from God's sight. Everything is uncovered and
> laid bare before the eyes of him to whom we must give account.
> (Heb. 4:12–13)

THIRTY YEARS LATER

- Even after more than thirty years of teaching, discipling, mentoring, and speaking, I'm still awed by the inherent power of Scripture itself—when confronted by a willing and open mind seeking God's truth—to instruct, convict, convince, and transform. I've read and written many books in that time but still find the practical exposition of Scripture is the most effective vehicle to impart God's timeless truth. That's the inspiration and conviction behind the devotional books I've written to guide people through the powerful process of praying Scripture back to God (e.g., *Handbook to Prayer, Handbook to Renewal, Face to Face,* and *Sacred Readings*).

- St. Irenaeus said: "Not only in this present age but in the Age to come, God will always have something more to teach man, and man will always have something more to learn from God."[6]

- The Bible isn't God's only revelation to the sons and daughters of Adam (Heb. 1:1-2), but it stands at the center, along with Christ, of the developing understanding in each Christian that reaches outward from there to embrace God.

EPILOGUE

W
e've frequently observed that certain biblical mysteries relate to others. Now we can go one step further: *Every* mystery relates to every other mystery. This is because God is the author of reality. In an *ultimate* sense, everything can be traced back to the person and plan of God. All the incomprehensibles revealed in Scripture connect together because they're the product of God's higher wisdom.

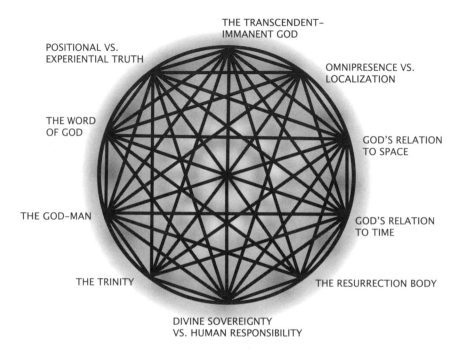

Begin with the God-man mystery and consider how it relates to each one of the others. Then go to the Trinity mystery and do the same, and so on in a counterclockwise direction, until you finally come back to the God-man mystery.

By this time it should be clear that we who are finite can't comprehend everything about the infinite God. But we *can* comprehend enough about God through his revelation to say meaningful things about him. The good news of salvation, for instance, has been so clearly communicated that even children can appropriate this message by receiving Christ as their personal Savior from sin.

> What, then, is my God? What, I ask, except the Lord *God? For who is Lord but the Lord? Or who is God save our God?* O highest and best, most powerful, most all-powerful, most merciful and most just, most deeply hidden and most nearly present, most beautiful and most strong, constant yet incomprehensible, changeless, yet changing all things, never new, never old, making all things new; *bringing the proud to decay and they know it not;* always acting and

always at rest; still gathering yet never wanting; upholding, filling
and protecting, creating, nourishing, and bringing to perfection;
seeking, although in need of nothing. You love, but with no storm
of passion; You are jealous, but with no anxious fear; You repent,
but do not grieve; in Your anger calm; You change Your works, but
never change Your plan; You take back what You find and yet have
never lost; never in need, You are yet glad of gain; never greedy, yet
still demanding profit on Your loans; to be paid in excess, so that
You may be the debtor, and yet who has anything which is not
Yours? You pay back debts which You never owed and cancel debts
without losing anything. And in all this what have I said, my God,
my Life, my holy sweetness? What does any man succeed in saying
when he attempts to speak of You? Yet woe to those who do not
speak of You at all, when those who speak most say nothing.[1]

Great is our Lord and mighty in power;
his understanding has no limit. (Ps. 147:5)

THIRTY YEARS LATER

- The sphere illustration underscores the unity and diversity of
  revealed truth. For example, the God-man mystery clearly relates
  to the mystery of the Trinity; the second person of the Godhead
  took humanity into himself, entered space-time history, lived in
  the power of the Spirit in obedience to the will of the Father, and
  now intercedes for us before the Father. It relates to divine sovereignty versus human responsibility in that it unites God's majesty
  with man's condition. It relates to the resurrection body since
  there's a resurrected man in heaven who is both the Lion and the
  Lamb. It relates to God's relation to time in that the eternal Alpha
  and Omega experienced the conditions and limitations of being
  embedded in the temporal. It relates to God's relation to space
  since the One who created the cosmos and holds it together personally entered into that cosmos. It relates to omnipresence
  versus localization because the God-man is present everywhere
  yet localized in a resurrected body. It relates to the transcendent-
  immanent God in that the awesome Pantocrator (the Ruler of all
  things) personally indwells those who trust in him. It relates to

positional versus experiential truth in that we dwell in the heavenly places in Christ Jesus and dwell in the world in which he manifests his life in and through us as we abide in him. And it relates to the mystery of the Word of God since he perfectly combines the divine and the human.

- This brief and incomplete sketch of the implications of the mystery of the God-man in relation to the other biblical mysteries illustrates how we can move on to each mystery in turn and relate it to all the others. "For from Him and through Him and to Him are all things. To him be the glory forever. Amen." (Rom. 11:36 NASB)

Notes

CHAPTER 2
THE GOD-MAN

1. This problem of the eternal generation of the Son from the Father represents a unique situation, if not another mystery. Some passages that show that Christ was the Son of God prior to his incarnation are Psalm 2:7; Isaiah 9:6; John 3:16–17; and Galatians 4:4. The nature of this sonship and "generation" are clearly unique and relate to the mystery of time (see chapter 7).

2. Søren Kierkegaard, *Concluding Unscientific Postscript*, trans. David F. Swenson and Walter Lowrie (Princeton: Princeton University Press. 1941), 480; David F. Swenson and Howard V. Hong, trans., *Philosophical Fragments* (Princeton: Princeton University Press, 1936, 1962), 46–47; S. U. Zuidema, *Kierkegaard* (Philadelphia: Presbyterian and Reformed Publishing Company, 1960).

CHAPTER 3
THE TRINITY

1. David H. Freeman, *Tillich* (Philadelphia: Presbyterian and Reformed Publishing Company, 1962), 10ff.

2. John F. Walvoord, in *Jesus Christ Our Lord* (Chicago: Moody Press, 1969), 51–54, shows that the Angel of the Lord, who appears many times in the Old Testament, is a theophany of the preincarnate Christ.

3. B. B. Warfield, "Trinity," *The International Standard Bible Encyclopedia*, James Orr, ed., 5 vols. (Grand Rapids, MI: Wm. B. Eerdmans Publishing Co., 1939), V, 3012.

4. R. A. Finlayson, "Trinity," *The New Bible Dictionary*, J. D. Douglas, ed., (Grand Rapids, MI: Wm. B. Eerdmans Publishing Co., 1962), 1300.

5. Henry M. Morris, *The Bible and Modern Science* (Chicago: Moody Press, 1951), 24–25.

6. Henry M. Morris, *Biblical Cosmology and Modern Science* (Nutley, NJ: Craig Press, 1970), 40.

7. Walter Martin, *The Kingdom of the Cults* (Minneapolis: Bethany Fellowship, 1965), 47.

8. Ibid., 178. Mormonism is actually polytheistic since it indicates there are other gods besides these three.

9. Hinduism is a pantheistic religion since it teaches that everything, including good and evil, is God. This particular group of three gods is really symbolic of the being, becoming, and dissolution of the universe, a process that continues on and on in unlimited cycles.

10. Finlayson, "Trinity," 1300.

CHAPTER 4
DIVINE SOVEREIGNTY VS. HUMAN RESPONSIBILITY (SALVATION)

1. Lewis Carroll, *The Annotated Alice* (New York: Clarkson N. Potter, 1960), 251.

2. Other passages that support divine election and sovereignty include Ex. 14:17; Deut. 29:4; 32:39; 1 Sam. 2:25; 9:15—10:9; 2 Sam. 12:11; 1 Kings 22:23; Job 14:5; 38:1—42:3; Ps. 33:10–11; 47:7–8; 75:6–8; 102:18; 104:1–35; 139:16; Isa. 14:24; 40:12–26; 53:10; 55:11; Jer. 10:23; 15:2; Dan. 2:21; 4:17; Amos 4:7; Matt. 10:29–30; Luke 10:21; Acts 13:48; Rom. 8:29–30; Eph. 3:11; 2 Tim. 1:9; Rev. 17:17.

3. J. I. Packer, *Evangelism and the Sovereignty of God* (Chicago: InterVarsity Press, 1967), 22. Compare James 4:12.

4. Ibid., 23 (italics his).

5. Also compare Matthew 24:25–34 (esp. v. 31); John 6:44, 65; Acts 13:48 ("and all who were appointed for eternal life believed"); 16:14; Ephesians 1:4–5, 11; 2 Thessalonians 2:13; 1 Peter 1:1–2; Revelation 17:8.

6. John R. W. Stott, *Basic Christianity* (Downers Grove, IL: InterVarsity Press, 1958), 94.

7. Other passages that emphasize the human responsibility to respond to the offer

of salvation include Acts 13:38–39; Romans 1:16, 3:22, 26, 28; 4:5; 10:9–10; Galatians 3:22; Revelation 3:20.

8. John Warwick Montgomery, *Where Is History Going?* (Minneapolis: Bethany Fellowship, 1969), 160.

9. Kenneth G. Howkins, *The Challenge of Religious Studies* (Downers Grove, IL: InterVarsity Press, 1972), 24.

10. Jay E. Adams, *Competent to Counsel* (Philadelphia: Presbyterian and Reformed Publishing Company, 1970), 6.

CHAPTER 5
DIVINE SOVEREIGNTY VS. HUMAN RESPONSIBILITY (EVIL)

1. This term comes from Hugh Silvester's book *Arguing with God* (Downers Grove, IL: InterVarsity Press, 1971). This book, along with Edward J. Carnell's *An Introduction to Christian Apologetics* (Grand Rapids, MI: Wm. B. Eerdmans Publishing Co., 1948) is helpful in dealing with the problem of evil. Also see John W. Wenham, *The Goodness of God* (Downers Grove, IL: InterVarsity Press, 1974).

2. Compare Gleason L. Archer, Jr., *A Survey of Old Testament Introduction* (Chicago: Moody Press, 1964), 182, n. 10.

3. Silvester, *Arguing*, 36.

4. Carnell, *Apologetics*, 277.

5. Ibid., 302.

6. Robert D. Culver, "The Nature and Origin of Evil," *Bibliotheca Sacra*, CXXIX (April–June 1972), 108.

7. Clark H. Pinnock, "The Moral Argument for Christian Theism," *Bibliotheca Sacra*, CXXXXI (April–June 1974), 117.

8. C. S. Lewis, "De Futilitate" in *Christian Reflections*, Walter Hooper, ed. (Grand Rapids: Wm. B. Eerdmans Publishing Co., 1967), 69–70.

9. See Kenneth Boa and Larry Moody, *I'm Glad You Asked* (Wheaton, IL: Victor Books, 1982), 102–25; Norman L. Geisler, *Philosophy of Religion* (Grand Rapids: Zondervan, 1974), 311–403; and *The Roots of Evil* (Grand Rapids: Zondervan, 1978).

10. Francis Schaeffer, *Pollution and the Death of Man* (Wheaton, IL: Tyndale House Publishers, 1970), 31–32.

11. Carnell, *Apologetics*, 295 (italics his).

12. Erwin W. Lutzer, *The Morality Gap* (Chicago: Moody Press, 1972), 102 (n).

13. C. S. Lewis, *The Problem of Pain* (New York: The Macmillan Company, 1962), 127–28 (italics his).

CHAPTER 6
THE RESURRECTION BODY

1. The Septuagint translates Psalm 16:9–11 in a way that speaks more directly of the hope of the resurrection from the dead, and Peter quotes this version of the psalm as a prophecy of Christ's resurrection in Acts 2:25–32.

2. The Bible says little about the resurrection bodies of unbelievers. We know they will be resurrected (Dan. 12:2; John 5:28–29; Acts 24:15), but their bodies evidently will not be glorified (Dan. 12:2). The characteristics of Christ's risen body cannot be applied to theirs, and neither can the descriptions of 1 Corinthians 15. They will be cast into the lake of fire (Rev. 20:11–15) in their resurrected bodies.

3. J. A. Schep, *The Nature of the Resurrection Body* (Grand Rapids: Wm B. Eerdmans Publishing Co., 1964), 136.

4. Michael Green, *Man Alive* (Downers Grove, IL: InterVarsity Press, 1972), 82.

5. Alfred Edersheim, *The Life and Times of Jesus the Messiah* (London: Longmans, Green, and Co., 1886), II, 398–99.

6. Woody Allen, "My Speech to the Graduates," in *Side Effects* (New York: Ballentine Books, 1986).

CHAPTER 7
TIME

1. The only way a neutrino can be stopped is by a direct collision with other elementary particles. Such collisions are extremely unlikely, but they do occur because of the terrific number of neutrinos that pass through the earth at all times.

2. Edward F. Hills, *Space Age Science* (Des Moines, IA: The Christian Research Press, 1964), 122.

3. Lincoln Barnett, *The Universe and Dr. Einstein*, 2nd rev. ed. (New York: Harper & Row, 1948), 46–47. In a way, Aristotle anticipated this idea when he

suggested that if other heavens exist they must have their own time, meaning there would be many times at the same time.

4. James Reid, *God, the Atom, and the Universe* (Grand Rapids: Zondervan, 1968), 61–63.

5. Ibid., 64.

6. George Garrow, *One, Two, Three … Infinity* (New York: Viking Press, 1947), 105.

7. Another nasty theoretical effect of exceeding the speed of light is that time would be converted into space and space into time (Hills, *Space Age Science*, 32).

8. For instance, "At the speed of light one would weigh more than the universe, but be too small to measure, and would live forever, in no time!" (Reid, *God, Atom, Universe*, 70).

9. J. B. Priestly, *Man and Time* (New York: Crescent Books, 1964).

10. John Warwick Montgomery, *Principalities and Powers* (Minneapolis: Bethany Fellowship, 1973), 125.

11. J. B. Priestly, *Man and Time*, 292.

12. Charles Caldwell Ryrie, *A Survey of Bible Doctrine* (Chicago: Moody Press, 1972), 23.

13. John C. Whitcomb, Jr., adds that in God's creative work "it is impossible to imagine a time interval in the transition from nonexistence to existence! … At one moment there was no light; the next moment there was!" (*The Early Earth* [Grand Rapids: Baker Book House, 1972], 25). One interesting thing along this line comes from Genesis 1:14–19. If the passage is taken in its normal sense (that is, "day" equals a twenty-four-hour period; see Ex. 20:11), it means that God created not only the stars but also the light from the stars to the earth. In this interpretation, light from a star one billion light-years away isn't necessarily one billion years old. It would only be as old as the interval from the fourth day of creation until now, even though it has an appearance of greater age.

14. A. W. Tozer, *The Divine Conquest* (Harrisburg, PA.: Christian Publications, 1950), 21.

15. Martin Gardner, "Can Time Go Backward?" *Scientific American*, January 1967, 108.

16. C. S. Lewis, "On 'Special Providences,'" Appendix B of *Miracles*, in *The Best of C. S. Lewis* (New York: The Iversen Associates, 1969), 375. Incidentally, Lewis makes an interesting observation on the subject of time and prayer on the next page: "Most of our prayers if fully analysed, ask either for a miracle or for events

whose foundation will have to have been laid before I was born, indeed, laid when the universe began" (ibid., 376). Lewis goes on to conclude that a prayer at noon could become a contributing cause of an event that occurred two hours earlier (ibid., 377–379).

17. F. Duane Lindsey, "Essays Toward a Theology of Beauty, Part I: God Is Beautiful," *Bibliotheca Sacra*, CXXXI (April–June 1974), 134.

18. C. S. Lewis, "Historicism," in *Christian Reflections*, Walter Hooper, ed. (Grand Rapids, MI: William B. Eerdmans Publishing Co., 1967), 113.

19. Joseph Campbell, "On Mystic Shapes of Thing to Come—Circular and Linear," *Horizon*, 1974, 35. Priestly, *Man and Time*, 172. Geoffrey Parrinder, *A Dictionary of Non-Christian Religions* (Philadelphia: The Westminster Press, 1971).

20. J. R. R. Tolkien, *The Fellowship of the Ring*, 2nd ed. (Boston: Houghton Mifflin Company, 1965), 243. See John W. Montgomery, et. al., *Myth Allegory and Gospel* (Minneapolis: Bethany Fellowship, 1974), 127–129.

21. C. S. Lewis, *The Lion, the Witch and the Wardrobe* (New York: The Macmillan Company, 1950). Just the opposite effect can be found in Lord Dunsany's *The King of Elfland's Daughter* (New York: Ballantine Books, 1969), 28. In this fantasy, Alveric, a prince from our world, goes into a twilight world named Elfland for less than a day. When he returns, everyone is ten to twelve years older.

22. Oscar Cullmann, *Christ and Time* (Philadelphia: The Westminster Press, 1964), 46.

23. Ibid., 63.

24. Schep, *Resurrection Body*, 216.

25. A. W. Tozer, *The Knowledge of the Holy* (New York: Harper & Row, 1961), 52–53.

CHAPTER 8
SPACE (THE CREATION)

1. Arthur Koestler, *The Roots of Coincidence* (New York: Random House, 1972), 50–53.

2. Barnett, *The Universe*, 29.

3. Koestler, *Roots*, 57.

4. George Gamow, *One, Two, Three ... Infinity* (New York: Viking Press, 1947), 100. The three changes that relativistic speeds bring about are (1) dilation of time, (2) contraction of space, and (3) increase in mass.

5. Barnett, *The Universe*, 85.

6. "Calculations show that an object as dense as a neutron star must also have prodigiously concentrated gravity—a hundred billion times that of earth. So strong is the gravitational pull that a neutron-star mountain could rise no more than an inch, and to climb it would take more energy than your metabolism can create in a lifetime" (Kenneth F. Weaver, "The Incredible Universe," *National Geographic*, May 1974, 618).

7. This assumes that the universe isn't pulsating (expanding and contracting) endlessly and that matter is not infinitely old if it existed before the big bang.

8. See Barnett, *The Universe*, 106; and Oscar L. Brauer, "God of the Universe Watching Over the Earth," *Creation Research Society Quarterly*, January 1967, 7.

9. See Gamow, *Infinity*, 297–298; and Max Born, *Einstein's Theory of Relativity* (New York: Dover Publications, 1962), 345.

10. The biblical support of this important fact is impressive. Other references that clearly teach that God is the Creator of all that exists are Genesis 2:1; Exodus 20:11; 31:17; 2 Kings 19:15; 1 Chronicles 16:26; 2 Chronicles 2:12; Nehemiah 9:6; Job 9:8–9; 26:7; 38:4–7; Psalms 8:3; 19:1; 89:11; 90:2; 95:5; 102:25; 104; 121:2; 124:8; 134:3; 136:5–7; 146:6; 148:5; Isaiah 40:26, 28; 45:18; Jeremiah 27:5; 32:17; 33:2; 51:15; Amos 4:13; 9:6; Jonah 1:9; Zechariah 12:1; Mark 13:19; John 1:3, 10; Acts 14:15; 17:24; Romans 1:19–20; 1 Corinthians 8:6; Ephesians 3:9; Colossians 1:16; Hebrews 1:2, 10; 2:10; 2 Peter 3:5; Revelation 4:11; 10:6; 14:7.

11. James F. Coppedge, *Evolution: Possible or Impossible?* (Grand Rapids: Zondervan, 1973), 208–211, includes many speculations about the location of heaven and hell. Four of his guesses are (1) Hell may relate to the places of zero volume caused by gravitational collapse predicted by Penrose's theorem. (2) Two things could occupy the same space (he cites the empty space in atoms). We may not be able to detect the other realm even though it is coincident with our own. (3) Hell may be inside some black hole. (4) Heaven and hell may be too distant for detection (Coppedge, therefore, considers the possibility of instant space travel). However, the addition of another spatial dimension rather than placing heaven and hell in three-dimensional space seems to be a more satisfactory concept (see 1 Kings 8:27; 2 Cor. 12:2). Reid, *God, Atom, Universe*, 81 observes: "One more dimension would provide mankind with an unlimited heaven(s) which might be reached by simply stepping out or up, into the next dimension."

12. Tozer, *Knowledge*, 33–34.

13. Arthur G. Clarke, *Analytical Studies in the Psalms* (Kilmarnock, Scotland: John Ritchie Ltd., 1949), 66.

Chapter 9
Space (Omnipresence vs. Localization)

1. Lewis Sperry Chafer, *Systematic Theology*, vol. 1 (Dallas: Dallas Seminary Press, 1947), 221.

2. Rex Warner, trans., *The Confessions of St. Augustine* (New York: The New American Library, 1963), 18–19.

3. See John Warwick Montgomery's critique of pantheism in *Christianity for the Tough Minded* (Minneapolis: Bethany Fellowship, Inc. 1973), 21–22. Montgomery states: "Pantheism … is neither true nor false; it is something much worse, viz., entirely trivial. We had little doubt that the universe was here anyway; by giving it a new name ('God') we explain nothing. We actually commit the venerable intellectual sin of Word Magic, wherein the naming of the something is supposed to give added power either to the thing named or to the semantic magician himself" (ibid., 22).

4. Hildebert of Lavardin, cited in Tozer, *Knowledge*, 80.

5. A. W. Tozer, *The Pursuit of God* (Harrisburg, PA: Christian Publications, Inc. 1948), 35.

6. John continues to say that "even those who pierced him" will see him at the second advent (Rev. 1:7; see Zech. 12:10; John 19:37). Evidently, the "every eye" that will see him includes not only those who are on earth at that time but all creatures. The currently popular idea that all people will be able to see Christ when he comes through *television* is sheer nonsense unless those in hades have access to cable TV. Besides, a quick look at the destruction caused by the seal, trumpet, and bowl judgments in Revelation makes it clear that by the end of the tribulation when the second coming occurs, few people will still be watching television, even if the stations are transmitting (see Matt. 24:21–22). Christ compared his coming to lightning flashing from the east to the west (Matt. 24:27; Luke 17:24).

Chapter 10
The Transcendent-Immanent God

1. Louis Berkhof, *Systematic Theology* (Grand Rapids: Wm. B. Eerdmans Publishing Co., 1939), 29–34.

2. Stott, *Basic Christianity*, 73.

3. Cornelius Van Til, *The New Modernism*, 3rd ed. (Nutley, NJ: Presbyterian and

Reformed Publishing Company, 1946), 4–7. However, they also denied the idea of a temporal creation, and this logically leads to a God who isn't so transcendent after all. Van Til says: "Accordingly the transcendence doctrine of one who rejects casual creation cannot be that of a God who is really free. It must always be the transcendence of a God who is necessarily related to the universe" (ibid., 6–7).

4. Rem B. Edwards, *Reason and Religion* (New York: Harcourt Brace Jovanovich, Inc. 1972), 211. See also Ewert H. Cousines, ed., *Process Theology* (New York: Newman Press, 1971).

5. As Berkhof (*Systematic Theology*, 29–30) notes, Hegel and Schleiermacher also fit into the immanence extreme since they played down God's transcendence and denied revelation. They essentially said that all one needs to know about God can be discovered in the depths of one's being.

6. Robert E. Morosco, "Theological Implications of Fear: The Grasshopper Complex," *Journal of Psychology and Theology*, I (April 1973), 44.

7. Tozer, *Knowledge*, 77. Morosco ("Theological Implications," 50) gives a scriptural list of positive effects from the fear of God. Some of these include wisdom, happiness, displeasure with evil, and righteousness.

8. Kenneth Grahame, *The Wind in the Willows* (New York: Charles Scribner's Sons, 1933), 127.

Chapter 11
Positional vs. Experiential Truth

1. The list is set forth by Lewis Sperry Chafer in a section called "The Riches of Divine Grace" in his *Systematic Theology*, 234–265.

2. Another difference relates to sanctification. On one hand, believers are positionally sanctified; they've been *completely* set apart from the world to God in their position in Christ. But on the other hand, there's an experiential or progressive sense of sanctification, a *process* that continues throughout a believer's life and relates to his growth in the Lord. In the normal Christian life, experience should come gradually closer to position.

Chapter 12
The Word of God

1. Ryrie, *Bible Doctrine*, 38.

2. Norman L. Geisler and William E. Nix, *A General Introduction to the Bible* (Chicago: Moody Press, 1968), 27.

3. We don't know why God has allowed textual variants to creep into the manuscripts. No doubt the original manuscripts would be worshipped had they been preserved. God has chosen to use frail and fallible men to preserve his revelation, but at the same time his providence ensured the text remained free of serious corruption. Because of the quantity and quality of the manuscripts, textual criticism can be applied in the virtual reconstruction of the original text.

4. One place where this analogy breaks down is that Christ was never corrupted, but the Bible has been partly corrupted by impurities that entered the text. As we said before, however, we can still reconstruct the text to a point of substantial purity using textual criticism.

5. Tozer, *Divine Conquest*, 79.

6. Irenaeus, *Irenaeus Against Heresies* (Whitefish, MT: Kessinger Publishing, 2004), 3.

Epilogue

1. Augustine, Confessions, 1.4.

Thirty Years Later

- Obviously, a book written more than thirty years ago will use a substantially different and more limited set of resources than those available today. There has been an explosion in religious publishing in the last three decades, and we're privileged today to have access to more resources than anyone could have imagined in the past, particularly if we include the Internet. However, many authors quoted in this book have written timeless spiritual classics that will never be supplanted.

- Millennia ago, Qoheleth wrote, "The words of wise men are like goads, and masters of these collections are like well-driven nails; they are given by one Shepherd" (Eccl. 12:11 NASB). But he continued, "But beyond this, my son, be warned: the writing of many books is endless, and excessive devotion to books is wearying to the body" (v. 12 NASB). Books can be good servants but poor masters. They must be read with discernment, in the spirit of the Bereans who "received the word with great eagerness, examining the Scriptures daily to see whether these things were so" (Acts 17:11 NASB). All truth is from God, and, as believers, we must put the things we learn in all disciplines in context with the Lord of truth.